WRITE TO LEARN

A GUIDE TO WRITING ACROSS THE CURRICULUM

Margot K. Soven

LaSalle University

SOUTH-WESTERN College Publishing

An International Thomson Publishing Company

Copyright © 1996
by South-Western College Publishing
Cincinnati, Ohio

I(T)P

International Thomson Publishing
South-Western College Publishig is an ITP Company. The ITP trademark is used under license.

ISBN: 0-538-85991-1

1 2 3 4 5 6 MA 0 9 8 7 6 5

Printed in the United States of America.

Library of Congress Cataloging-in-Publication Data

Soven, Margot.
    Write to learn: a guide to writing across the curriculum/Margot K. Soven.
        p.   cm.
    Includes bibliographical references.
    ISBN 0-538-85991-1   (alk. paper)
    1. English language—Rhetoric—Study and teaching.
2. Interdisciplinary approach in education.   **I.** Title.
PE1404.S685   1995   95-30922
808'.042'071—dc20   CIP

Acquisitions Editor: Randy G. Haubner
Production Editor: Crystal Chapin
Production House: DPS Associates, Inc.
Cover Design: Michael H. Stratton
Internal Design: Russell Schneck Design
Marketing Manager: Stephen E. Momper

INTRODUCTION

"You are a graduate student in English who has been assigned to teach freshman composition."

"You are a graduate student in history assigned to teach a writing-intensive freshman seminar in history."

"You are a biology instructor who would like to use writing more effectively to teach the subject matter of your discipline."

"You are an undergraduate English-Education major preparing to teach high school writing."

What kinds of writing will you assign? What kinds of assignments will help you teach the course material? How will you encourage students to plan, draft, and revise? How will you give students meaningful feedback?

This text responds to these questions. Teachers in all disciplines, graduate students planning to teach, and undergraduates training to be teachers will find this handbook useful. Its contents are based on my twelve years of experience as writing across the curriculum coordinator and director of freshman composition at La Salle University, and my more than twenty years experience teaching writing and English-methods courses on both the undergraduate and graduate level. The assignments in the handbook have been contributed by teachers in the humanities, social sciences, natural sciences, business, and nursing.

This text proposes a rhetorical approach to writing instruction which emphasizes adapting content, form, and style to the purpose and audience for writing. It underscores the importance of writing assignments as the blueprints of a writing program in both composition and noncomposition courses. A well-constructed assignment provides a plan for the instructor and the student: for the instructor it is a guide for planning instruction students need to execute the assignment effectively and for evaluating their papers; for the student the assignment defines thinking tasks and manuscript conventions, and it guides the writing process. Experience tells us that students write most successfully when they have a clear understanding of the purpose of each and audience for each assignment, the tasks required, and the criteria the teacher will use to evaluate their papers.

This book is in four parts: Chapter 1: Planning and Evaluating Writing Assignments; Chapter 2: Instructions and Models for Academic Assignments; Chapter 3: Teaching Materials, and Chapter 4: Designing a Comprehensive Writing Program. Chapter 1 presents a rationale for "writing across the curriculum" and describes general principles of assignment construction that apply to all disciplines and assignments on the secondary and college level. Chapter 2 offers brief descriptions of commonly assigned papers and accompanying samples to help instructors learn how to develop clear instructions and evaluation criteria for a variety of assignment types. Chapter 3 includes student materials that can be adapted for individual classroom use, and Chapter 4 discusses a comprehensive approach to designing writing programs, using La Salle University's writing program as an example.

Margot K. Soven
Writing Project Coordinator
La Salle University

ACKNOWLEDGMENTS

This text would not have been possible without the vigorous participation of faculty and students in my English-methods courses and faculty summer workshops. I thank them all for their good ideas, and I especially thank those faculty who went through their files to provide me with sample assignments.

In addition, I thank Bro. Joseph F. Burke, F.S.C., President of La Salle University, Dr. Joseph A. Kane, provost, and Dr. Barbara C. Millard, Dean of the School of Arts and Sciences for their continued support of the Writing Project's activities. I also thank Bro. James Muldoon, F.S.C., former Dean of the School of Arts and Sciences and Emery C. Mollenhauer, F.S.C. for their encouragement during the early years of the Writing Project. My special thanks to Dr. James A. Butler, Chair of the English Department, and Ms. Francine J. Lottier, the English Department Secretary, whose assistance to the Writing Project is invaluable. I am especially grateful to Ms. Lottier for typing the final manuscript of this text.

TABLE OF CONTENTS

Chapter 3: Teaching Materials and Student Handouts

Chapter 4: Designing a Comprehensive Writing Program

WHAT IS "WRITING ACROSS THE CURRICULUM"?

As educated adults we readily acknowledge the significance of writing in our own lives. We not only write letters of inquiry and complaint and messages of warmth and cheer, but we write to participate in the community of discourse of our disciplines. Perhaps even more important, when we are puzzled, we write to clarify our thoughts; we take notes; we write notes to ourselves. We write to solve problems. We write for professional, practical, and personal reasons and know that the ability to write gives us a sense of power in each of these domains. We write, in other words, to learn as well to communicate what we have learned. We believe it is important to transmit these skills to our students and struggle to find methods for encouraging students to write in purposeful ways in our classes, hoping that they too will learn to use writing in their personal and professional lives.

"Writing Across the Curriculum" then is more than just another educational fad or a new buzz phrase. It reflects a point of view as well as a set of teaching practices. Its advocates believe that (1) writing is important as a tool for learning, an aid to clarify thinking, as well as a vital communication skill, and (2) that all teachers, not just language arts or English department faculty, should share the responsibility of helping students realize that writing is not just a necessary skill in college and an advantageous skill in work, but that we write "to organize our lives, necessary functions of living in societies" (Lindemann 6).

In recent years there has been a great deal of interest in using writing as a means of facilitating learning in school. A review of the literature on this subject suggests that there are nine reasons that might be advanced for such a practice:

1. The act of writing enhances knowing: retrieving information, organizing it, and expressing it in writing seems to improve understanding and retention.

2. Writing is an active learning process, and active learning seems to be more effective than passive reception.

3. Writing is a way of making knowledge personal. The writer brings to bear a subjective point of view and reinterprets personally what has been learned.

4. Writing focuses attention: those who know they are expected to write tend to be more attentive.

5. Writing seems to facilitate thinking about a subject. The act of writing enables the writer to discern new relationships and make new connections.

6. Writing is a way of sharing what is known. Students can use writing to share with classmates what they have learned.

7. Writing provides immediate feedback to the learner and to the teacher about what has been learned—and what has not been learned.

8. Writing is a self-paced mode of learning; the pace of writing seems to match better the pace of learning, slowing down the process of those who might be inclined to finish a learning task too quickly.

9. Each discipline has its own way of knowing and its own modes of communicating knowledge; students should have a broad knowledge of how writing is used in several diverse disciplines. For example, a scientist reporting the results of a scientific inquiry uses objective language to communicate results; a literary critic evaluating a novel uses more subjective language to discuss personal reactions.

The teaching methods advocated by the writing across the curriculum movement help us to connect in the best possible way our concern for teaching our disciplines with our interest in helping our students see the importance of writing, because these methods show us how we can exploit writing to teach the content of our courses more effectively. Writing that is consciously related to course objectives gives students a chance to learn the content of that course in a more active way than simply by speaking or reading about it (Emig 27).

The aim of this manual is to present these methods. We can teach our disciplines and help our students improve their writing, using methods of designing and evaluating assignments that many teachers have found useful, without making impractical demands on our students or ourselves.

CHAPTER 1

Planning and Evaluating Writing Assignments

CONSTRUCTING WRITING ASSIGNMENTS: SOME GENERAL PRINCIPLES

A good writing assignment is related to the learning objectives of the course, is clearly presented, and is manageable for both student and teacher. Richard Larson's advice about planning assignments for composition courses seems to apply equally well to noncomposition courses:

> . . . a theme assignment ought not to be given simply to evoke an essay to be judged. Its purpose should be to teach, to give students an experience in composing, selecting, arranging and expressing thoughts from which they can learn as much as from the reaction of the teacher to the essay. The very act of writing the assignment should help students think a little more incisively, reason a little more soundly and write a little more effectively than they did before encountering it ("Teaching" 209).

A good assignment aids instruction while a poor one detracts from it. Research indicates that a casually constructed or poorly developed assignment places every student under a needless handicap and guarantees that a sizable fraction of the papers will be defective (Larson, "Teaching" 210). The following suggestions are offered to help you develop assignments that provide useful opportunities for learning as well as to enhance the possibility of your receiving good student papers.

1. Relate the assignment to course objectives.

Before drafting an assignment, review the objectives for the course. Then consciously design the assignment to help your students achieve one or more of these objectives. Assignments can help reinforce course objectives, such as understanding relationships, becoming familiar with new terminology or concepts, and applying concepts to particular problems. For example, if a major purpose of the course is to teach students how to read the texts of the discipline (often the case in introductory courses), assignments that require students to summarize readings may be very appropriate.

Assignments clearly tied to course objectives seem purposeful to students. They realize that the time they spend on writing their papers is time well spent.

2. Construct assignments that require original thinking about significant issues.

Before deciding on a subject and task for an assignment, ask yourself, "Will the assignment encourage students to make some new discovery about themselves, their environment, a text or some other significant object of inquiry?" If, for example, the content of readings is very abstract and difficult to comprehend (as is often the case in a philosophy course, for example), an assignment requiring students to synthesize their notes from class and readings may serve this purpose. "Original" ideas can include those new to the writer even though they may be familiar to the teacher (Britton, et al. 31).

3. Specify a purpose and audience for writing.

Present the assignment task (comparison, summary, etc.) in "rhetorical context." Research seems to suggest that we can anticipate better writing when students can imagine a real situation where that writing can be used. For example, instead of "compare and contrast WWI and WWII," a writing assignment framed within a rhetorical context would read, "You have been asked to explain the major differences between WWI and WWII to a group of high school students who have not yet studied this subject."

4. Specify the format of the paper.

Clearly indicate the genre (report, essay, etc.) for the assignment as well as other manuscript requirements, such as length. Although freedom to choose a format may be appropriate in advanced courses, students in introductory and intermediate courses seem to need format guidelines.

5. Specify evaluation criteria.

By telling students the criteria you will use to evaluate their work, you provide them with guidelines for judging their papers before they submit them. This practice may also help to focus your students' efforts on the major objectives of the assignment. Furthermore, clarifying the evaluation criteria when you develop the assignment can save time when you grade papers.

6. Leave some room for student choice.

Students seem more motivated to write when some of the decisions necessary for completing the writing task are left up to them. More advanced students can choose topics, purposes, and audiences for their writing as well as format.

Novice students are usually more comfortable when the choice is restricted. For example, the seminar student could be assigned to "pick a topic from those we are studying this semester and write a research paper" whereas the student in an introductory course might be asked to choose one of three topics suggested by the instructor.

CONSTRUCTING ASSIGNMENTS FOR TEACHING DISCOVERY

"Had I been blessed with even limited access to my own mind, there would be no reason to write. I write entirely to find out what I'm thinking, what I'm looking at, what I see and what it means" (Joan Didion).

Writing assignments can be classified according to their major purpose: assignments that both help students synthesize course material and test what they have learned (usually graded), and assignments that have as their sole purpose to help them learn course material (rarely graded).

The second type, often called informal writing, is the kind of writing people use to record and remember information, to discover and sort out ideas, and to reinforce learning. Informal writing can also be used to explore tentatively a subject from memory and to summarize and respond to ideas from readings and observations. Its personal idiom allows the student freedom for experimentation. Because many instructors are not familiar with informal writing, this section of the manual will focus on basic concerns such as the audience for informal writing, forms of informal writing, and evaluating informal writing.

Audience

Although instructors may choose to read their students' informal writing, the primary audiences for this writing are the students themselves, since its major function is not communication but self-clarification. In the case of informal writing, audiences other than the author are always eavesdroppers on the author's intellectual processes.

Forms

Informal writing can take various forms, such as logs, journals, and ungraded exercises, done in class or assigned for homework. Its content can be tightly or loosely controlled. When assignments are related to readings, students can be given questions or prompts, or they can be asked to write about whatever interests them or seems important. For example, a structured journal assignment about readings might include such questions as

- ◆ What is being assumed (taken for granted) in this passage?
- ◆ Does your experience lead you to accept the assumption?
- ◆ What would you need to do to confirm the statements made in this passage?

In contrast, instructions for an unstructured assignment might ask students to record their reactions, opinions, feelings, perceptions, intuitions, understandings, explanations, and questions.

In-Class Writing

Informal writing can be used in class to encourage active processing of the course material through active participation. Starting class by having students write a response to a question on the board may help them connect assigned readings or the previous lecture to the lecture of that day. To consolidate thinking during class, a lecture or discussion can be stopped at a critical point, and students can be asked to jot down the definition of a critical term in their own words or summarize the discussion. The teacher may say, for example, "Write for several minutes on the implication of that point."

During class, informal writing can also be used to record small group discussions, often an effective way to encourage quiet students to speak in class. The class is divided into small groups, each having either the same or different questions to consider. The group can report their written responses to the whole class or write part of this response on the board. Having the students write their responses eases the process of reviewing them and validates the importance of the discussion.

Out-of-Class Writing

Informal writing assigned for homework can encourage ongoing reflective thinking about and careful reading of course material. Students have said it also helps them to keep up with reading assignments.

Evaluating Informal Writing

Informal writing cannot be evaluated using the criteria designed for evaluating formal papers, since by its nature it is usually not revised. Furthermore, the loose organizational pattern of this writing typically reflects the chronology of the student's evolving thoughts rather than the needs of the reader. Some instructors may choose not to respond to it at all, merely checking to make sure that students have completed the assignment. Most instructors who assign journals seem to prefer to write comments about the content of the papers. Those who try to judge the quality of the journals seem to favor a check/check-plus system to identify adequate and superior work, although more research is needed to help us refine criteria for journal evaluation.

A word of caution and a word of encouragement:

Because most of our students are not familiar with informal writing, instructors need to discuss its value before assigning it. We need to offer clear guidelines as well as models of both professional writers' journals and former students' journals to help students get started. (For examples of such guidelines, see Chapter 2.)

CONSTRUCTING ASSIGNMENTS FOR TEACHING ACADEMIC WRITING

As opposed to informal writing that may be ongoing in various forms throughout the semester, formal writing is assigned at specific times. Also, in contrast to informal writing, formal writing is assigned to allow students to demonstrate their mastery of course content, as well as to give them an opportunity to learn the subject matter of the course through writing about it. Many instructors believe that students have not really mastered information and concepts until they can intelligently express that understanding in written form.

Formal writing teaches students the conventions of thinking and writing in college, since we judge that writing to a large extent by those conventions. Formal writing assignments can also teach students methods of gathering, developing, organizing, and reporting data acceptable to all disciplines as well as the specific application of these methods in different disciplines. Students learn that we are concerned not just with ideas but with the way they are explained and reported and that each discipline has its own rules for evaluating evidence as well as its own requirements for presenting that evidence.

Academic writing prizes detailed support of conclusions, logical argumentation, and clarity. However, the nature of that evidence, the lines of argument, and the genre and style of writing used to present it will often be unique to the discipline. For example, in the social sciences evidence often takes the form of detailed descriptions of human behavior; arguments are often situated in the institutional context, and the form often chosen for presenting the information is the report. In contrast, students in a literature class learn that evidence for their arguments usually lies within the text and the presentation form most appropriate is often the essay.

We need to make conscious efforts to construct formal assignments that make students aware of the unique nature of the content, the lines of reasoning, and the genres of writing particular to our disciplines, although many assignment types are appropriate across disciplines.

Assignment Forms

Especially in introductory courses, students can be assigned forms of writing common to all disciplines, such as the essay and book review. Discipline-specific forms, such as reports, can also be introduced in introductory courses when appropriate or delayed for advanced courses. Regardless of the type of writing assigned, it is useful to remember that short papers (3-5 pages) may be as effective as longer ones for teaching. A short research paper, for example, may teach students the processes for writing the research paper just as well as a longer one.

Sequencing

Formal assignments can be sequenced by changing any one or a combination of the following parts of an assignment:

- The purpose and audience (from familiar to less familiar).
- The nature (and/or number) of the thinking tasks (concrete to abstract).
- The kind and amount of data (concrete or abstract).
- The structure of the assignment (from structured to open-ended).
- The length.

The most effective kind of sequencing approach has not been established and may be different for different disciplines. For example, one could sequence writing about readings using the suggestions of Charles Bazerman. Bazerman's assignments cluster in three categories: assignments for expressing understanding of texts, assignments for evaluating texts, and assignments for developing original analyses and arguments based on primary research. Students progress from writing about one text to writing about many. Bazerman theorizes that students need to learn how to analyze, interpret, and evaluate one work before they can compare and synthesize the information from several works. Explicit models for Bazerman's assignments can be found in his text, *The Informed Writer*.

Library Assignments

Formal writing assignments can help to familiarize our students with library resources. These need not always take the form of the traditional research paper. For example, students can write critiques of journal articles, reviews of journals (an analysis of the content of a particular journal), or annotated bibliographies. Furthermore, research papers can range from highly structured assignments in introductory courses to assignments in advanced courses in which students choose their own topics, methods of research, and sources.

A Note on Length

Useful guidelines for tailoring the required length of the assignment to the content are offered by Maxine Hairston in *Successful Writing*:

- 3–5 pages: One major point articulated and supported.

   Example: the development of one character in a play or at the most the contrast of two characters. In an economics paper, the description of the unique features of one credit union.

- 8–10 pages: The implications of a limited thesis.

   Example: an effective comparison of the New York and Paris subway system or the effects on high schools of large numbers of dropouts.

PREPARING STUDENTS FOR WRITING ASSIGNMENTS

When we give a writing assignment we should ask ourselves four questions:

1. How much and what kinds of information should we use to fully explain the tasks and requirements of the assignment?

2. What are the skills necessary for the successful completion of the assignment?

3. Do these skills need to be taught or reviewed?

4. How much assistance will students need during the process of working on the assignment?

Assignment-related instruction includes the activities we choose in response to these questions.

Explaining the Assignment

Class time devoted to discussion and questions about the assignment seems important to the students even if the assignment has been distributed in written form. The instructor should make sure that students understand key terms, such as 'analyze', 'classify', or 'critique', as well as manuscript requirements. If evaluation criteria have been included, these too can be reviewed.

Model papers from previous semesters, distributed and analyzed in class, can clarify even further what's expected. If models are used, the subject matter of the assignment may be changed to avoid plagiarism. For example, a teacher interested in assigning the critique can choose a different reading each semester.

A word of caution: Some instructors believe that models restrict the student's approach to the assignment. They argue that the student, having seen the model, may not explore alternative methods for developing the material. This possible limitation should be weighed against the benefits of using models.

Teaching the Skills

The skills necessary for successfully accomplishing most college writing assignments range from data gathering and thinking skills to editing and documentation skills. In many cases, these skills are integrated in the course content. For example, in a sociology class students are taught interviewing techniques as an important part of the course subject matter. This same skill is needed for gathering information for a writing assignment. Similarly, in a philosophy class the lines of reasoning required by the writing assignment are practiced daily. Students learn to discuss issues and theories dialectically, similar to their task in the paper.

Special kinds of assignments will often require a review of the skills taught previously. For example, when we assign a library research paper, we may need to review methods for locating and using reference materials and for documenting their use. Similarly, prior to essay exams, a discussion of strategies for taking essay exams seems to have a significant positive effect on students' performance. If time permits, a practice question might be assigned. Student responses could then be evaluated and compared as part of a discussion about the characteristics of a good essay question response.

Encouraging a Process Approach: Prewriting

Many of our students start a writing assignment too close to the deadline for submitting the paper. Instructors can encourage students to execute the assignment in stages by aiding them during the prewriting, drafting, revision, and editing process. For example, we can teach students how to find topics in our disciplines and how to generate ideas. The news reporter's who-what-when-where-why is a useful heuristic for either narrowing a topic or collecting information. Another method such as freewriting (writing whatever you know about a subject without censoring your thoughts) works for some students. Questions like the following can teach students how to systematically choose a research paper topic:

> Choose a social issue and eventually narrow it to a specific, controversial problem. Research both sides of the controversy and report your conclusions.

They are then asked to complete the following exercise to find a topic:

- Define "social issue."
- List five social issues.
- Which one do you know the most about?
- Which one do you know the least about?
- Which one would you like to know more about? Why? (Possible reasons: the issue affects you personally; you already have strong views about this issue but would like to know what the other side has to say.)

Drafting and Revising: Outlines

Research on the writing process concludes that for most writers the writing process is recursive. When drafting or revising, we often return to the planning stage of writing. This cycle can be repeated many times. Therefore, while students should be encouraged to develop outlines to help them organize the material generated during the prewriting phase of composing, they should be urged to view outlines as working documents rather than rigid plans. Some students may find that writing a quick first draft is more useful than constructing an outline first. In this case, they can use the descriptive outline technique suggested by Kenneth Bruffee (*A Short Course in Writing* 36). Bruffee suggests writing a sentence describing the function of each paragraph in the draft to evaluate the ordering of ideas in the draft.

Drafting and Revising: Peer Review

Students can help each other revise their papers when they are given appropriate training and guidelines. Methods for training students should include a discussion about the reasons peer teaching is effective as well as the use of models and demonstration sessions. The video *Using Student Writing Groups* by Hale and Wyche-Smith introduces college students to a read-aloud method for peer review. Students listen to each paper twice and record their impressions in plus/minus/question mark columns, discussing their observations after each author reads. The film demonstrates good peer review etiquette, such as how to frame critical comments constructively and how to give positive as well as negative feedback. A more structured approach to peer review requires that students read each other's papers and make comments and suggestions with the aid of a checklist prepared by the instructor. The evaluation checklists in Chapter 2 can serve as useful models for peer review checklists. This checklist may include questions that apply to most kinds of writing.

For example,

- What is the main point of the essay?

- Do the details show this point clearly?

- Does the essay leave me with unanswered questions?

- What are the strengths of this essay?

- Are there any mechanical problems that hinder my reading?

A checklist may also include questions that apply to specific kinds of writing. For example students reviewing reports might be asked the following:

- Does the introduction include a statement of the problem?

- Is the analysis clear?

- Is the language of the report unbiased?

Students can also help each other with last minute proofreading and editing at the class session during which they submit their papers. This last check often saves them from being penalized for spelling and punctuation errors they do not catch themselves.

Peer review has two additional advantages: in addition to helping students to improve their papers, students learn to write for audiences besides the teacher, and they improve their ability to judge their own writing by having to evaluate another student's work. Instructors can evaluate the effectiveness of peer review by comparing drafts and final papers, reviewing student comments, and surveying student opinion about the value of the peer review process.

Drafting and Revising: The Instructor's Role

Instructors who want to help students while they are writing their papers need not read whole drafts, a time-consuming process. Students might be asked to submit a research plan, an outline, or the first paragraph of an essay if the instructor wants to check on what has been accomplished thus far and offer suggestions. One instructor has his students submit the analysis section of a report for review prior to completing the report, because in previous semesters students had difficulty with that part of the writing assignment. Another instructor has students submit an annotated bibliography as part of the process of writing the research paper.

Student-teacher conferences can serve as important alternatives to written feedback. Although instructors may worry about the time required to conduct these conferences, conferences may save time if they are held before final papers are submitted. Final copies often have fewer problems for the instructor to note when they are preceded by conferences. Students repeatedly affirm the value of personal, one-on-one conferences when asked to compare the benefits of alternative methods used for teaching writing. Effective conferencing (see Harris, *Teaching One to One: The Writing Conference*) requires that students help set the agenda for the conference and during the conference actively contribute to revising their papers.

EVALUATING AND RESPONDING TO STUDENT WRITING

We evaluate student writing for two purposes—to instruct and to assign grades. Using evaluation effectively for either purpose is not easy. It is often difficult to decide whether a piece of writing is effective and whether the objectives we have set for the paper have been achieved. Equally important, we face the problem of communicating our judgments to the students in a pedagogically useful way and deciding on the criteria to be used to grade an assignment. Furthermore, it's hard to give each paper adequate attention when faced with a large stack of papers and limited amounts of time. Conscientious, sensitive evaluation of our students' papers is both time-consuming and mentally taxing.

Noncomposition instructors need to deal with these issues, though their objectives for assigning writing are different from the objectives of the writing instructor. Whereas the writing instructor assigns writing to teach students how to write, other instructors assign writing primarily to teach the subject matter of their courses, and secondarily to help students improve their writing. Regardless of their goals for assigning writing, all instructors need to design evaluation systems that provide effective instruction, are fair to the students, and are practical to implement.

Teachers in many disciplines have found the following suggestions useful in designing such systems. They can be grouped into two categories: developing criteria and methods of communicating evaluations to the student.

1. Develop a limited set of criteria.

The "overgrading" syndrome has been the subject of much research. There seems to be no significant difference between the writing scores of students whose teachers marked their paper intensively and students whose teachers noted a few or moderate numbers of corrections. Students seem not to be able to cope with many error notations in a single paper. Therefore, evaluation criteria should probably be limited to five or six characteristics.

2. Criteria should reflect the special characteristics of the particular assignment.

Noncomposition teachers should focus evaluation on content. For example, to evaluate a case report in a sociology class, an instructor developed the following criteria:

a. Does the report provide a clear description of the client? (This includes not only the client's problem but how the client presented him/herself in therapy.)

b. Does the report do more than simply state what happened in the first session, second session, etc?

c. Does the report include an adequate summary?

d. If I were the next therapist for this client, would I have some idea as to what to try next or what to avoid from your report?

To evaluate the summary of a journal article an instructor used the following criteria:

a. Does the summary contain all major points?

b. Is the relationship between the points made clear?

c. Is the slant or bias of the article reflected in the summary?

Instructors using a writing assignment to teach students the forms of writing common to their discipline may want to add special criteria for form. For example, when evaluating review papers in a science class, the instructor included these categories:

- Logical format
- Appropriate headings
- Transitions
- Introduction
- Conclusion

Instructors who prefer to develop general criteria applicable to many kinds of writing assignments may find the following questions useful:

a. Is the writer addressing all parts of the assignment?

b. Is the main idea clear?

c. Is the main idea adequately developed and explained?

d. Are there logical connections among the various parts of the argument?

e. Does the writer show adequate understanding of technical vocabulary and concepts?

f. Is the paper free from mechanical errors (Holder and Moss 37)?

3. Criteria should include general qualities required for all assignments regardless of content or form.

Students need to be reminded that spelling, punctuation, and grammar and usage will always be taken into account, though the noncomposition instructor may place more importance on content in assigning a grade.

4. Develop a grading scale.

Although it is impossible to develop a mechanical formula for assigning grades, it is possible to describe a range of characteristics typical of papers that will receive specific grades. Developing such descriptions helps to avoid eccentricity of judgment that can occur when an instructor completely ignores or focuses too heavily on one element in the paper in assigning a grade. A grading scale for a Case Report paper included the following descriptions:

An "A" paper should include a clear statement of the purpose in the introduction; an account of the data unified by generalizations; an analysis of the data arranged in appropriate categories; paragraphs that reflect logic of content, correct spelling, punctuation, and grammar; and an appropriate manuscript.

The "B" paper should exhibit all the qualities of the "A" paper. However, one section, either the introduction or conclusion, may be flawed, or the analysis may not be as perceptive as the analysis in the "A" paper. Paragraphing must be correct most of the time, and there may be no more than five errors in sentence structure, spelling, or manuscript.

The "C" paper includes all the components of the Case Report; however, the analysis may not be sufficiently developed. The paper is thin. (Paragraphing, etc. same as in "B" paper)

The "D" paper does not contain all of the elements of the Case Report and contains many mechanical problems.

The "F" paper, also failing in content, includes egregious errors in all areas.

Developing a grading scale for a new assignment is difficult. However, a general description should be attempted with the expectation of refining the scale when the assignment is used in subsequent semesters.

5. Distribute criteria to students.

After many years of schooling, students expect their instructors to be vague about evaluation standards. However, both their writing and attitudes towards writing are bound to improve when grading standards are made explicit. When students talk about their worst writing experiences, they rank murky grading standards with vague, misleading assignments as a major cause of their dissatisfaction.

6. Respond to student writing.

The most time-consuming part of the evaluation process is the actual marking of papers, a writing problem in itself that entails difficult decisions about how and what to communicate. The content and form of our remarks depends on the goals of evaluation. If the goal is to have the student revise after evaluating a draft, comments may be more extensive than on the finished paper. It is well known that students pay more attention to comments on drafts than they do to comments on a paper that has already been graded. When responding to final papers we may have one or more of the following objectives:

a. To justify the grade.

b. To help students better understand course material.

c. To make them aware of a writing problem.

d. To prepare them for future assignments.

Regardless of the purpose, our responses to student papers should have the following characteristics:

a. Comments should be clearly stated in vocabulary familiar to the student. Try to avoid terse comments such as "awkward" and "unclear." For example, instead of "lacks development" one might say, "I do not have enough information to understand your point. You should have at least one more example."

b. Comments should encourage self-sufficiency. Since we will not "be there" in the future, students must learn to correct their own writing. Make suggestions and raise questions rather than correct the problem yourself. For example, the following question asks the student to reconsider the organization of the paper: "Did you consider placing the description of the house elsewhere in the paper?"

c. Comments should not be discouraging. When possible, stress the positive. A simple comment such as "good point" or "well expressed" can often inspire greater effort on the next assignment. When it is impossible to give unqualified praise, a comment such as "The beginning of a good idea" is appropriate on a paper that reflects hard work.

Include summary comments to show that you are interested in what the students have to say, as well as how they say it. Especially point out new information you have learned from the paper, when that is the case.

7. The form of response.

Comments in the margin: Instructors often write comments about content in the margin of the paper and include a summary comment on the last page. The advantage of this procedure is that comments are next to sections that are the subject of the comments. However, sometimes these comments are difficult to read and often mar the appearance of the paper to the point where the student is reluctant to read them.

Comments within the text: These should be limited for the most part to sentence level matters such as style, usage, mechanics, and spelling.

Checklists: An evaluation sheet, including a checklist of the evaluation criteria and ample room for a summary comment, may be more effective and efficient from the point of view of both instructor and student. The student gets a comprehensive view of the paper in one place. Instructors no longer write the same comments on each paper. For example, instead of writing, "You did not use sufficient sources," the instructor simply writes "No" beside the checklist category "Sufficient sources." Also, some instructors believe the checklist helps them to remain objective while reading a large number of papers. And finally, the evaluation sheet, unlike comments on the students' papers, can be discarded and replaced by another when the instructor wishes to revise his/her judgment of the paper.

CHAPTER 2

Instructions and Models for Academic Assignments

INTRODUCTION

Experience tells us that students write most successfully when they have a clear understanding of the purpose of the assignment and the tasks the assignment requires. These brief descriptions of commonly assigned papers may help you clarify instructions for papers you already assign and, perhaps, give you ideas for new assignments. Keep in mind that assignments rarely fit neatly into these categories; most assignments usually include elements characteristic of several of these types.

Sample assignments illustrate the assignment types. Several assignments by the same instructor were included to demonstrate how instructors employ a range of assignment types for different purposes. These assignments are not "perfect assignments" but were chosen because they represent several basic principles of assignment design.

This section also includes specific suggestions for introducing assignments and evaluating them. If instructors want to use such guides, they should modify them to suit their own assignments.

The suggestions and guides in this section are an outgrowth of discussions with faculty during the summer workshops as well as informal meetings during the academic year.

The following guides are included in this section:

- Introduction
- The Journal Assignment
- The Personal-Response Essay
- The Summary Essay
- The Critique and Book Reivew Essay
- The Short Analysis Essay
- The Argument Essay
- The Exploratory Essay
- The Research Paper and Review Essay
- The Report
- The Essay Exam

THE JOURNAL ASSIGNMENT

The Journal Defined

The journal, or log, one kind of informal writing, serves the general function in all disciplines of stimulating and structuring thinking about course material on a periodic basis. Journals become histories of evolving thought.

In addition to helping students learn course material, this kind of writing helps them "personalize" the subject matter. The journal is usually written in the first person about ideas important to the writer.

For example, Jonathan Griffiths, Chemistry Department, Stockton State College, requires a personal journal of students' experiences in the laboratory, noting that "Information is sterile unless given the personality of interpretation" (Kloss 14). Journals also help students reflect on their process of solving problems. The "process journal" has the two-fold purpose of making students self-conscious about the way they approach problems and offering the instructor a method of checking the class's progress. Beva Eastman, Mathematics Department, William Patterson College, has students keep a math log in which they record their questions about the course material. One student's entry begins, "I just don't understand how to get explicit formulas and recursion formulas" (Kloss 14). At La Salle, instructors use journals for a variety of purposes, such as to encourage students to react independently to required readings prior to coming to class (Hornum), and to structure the reading of related course materials (McNichol). In foreign language classes, the journal becomes a record of class exercises and notes for talks and compositions (Morocco).

Students' attitudes to journals are generally positive when they have a clear understanding of the purpose of the journal. In *Personality Dynamics and Adjustment* (Psychology 205), taught by Prof. Thomas McCarthy, when asked "Was one assignment in the course more purposeful than the others," most students cited the Adaptive Behavior Assignment. One student commented,

> "It made you think about yourself. We learned to think about our lives. When you are writing most papers, you simply want to get them done."

Journals are usually organized chronologically rather than thematically: the loose oganizational pattern of this writing reflects the pattern of the student's evolving thoughts. They are usually not revised. Entries are usually not written in formal academic prose, but instead, the writer uses a more personal, conversational style, since the focus is primarily on ideas rather than on presentation.

Evaluating Journals

Most instructors who assign journals prefer to write comments about the content rather than to assess them with a grade. A check/ check-plus system is sometimes used to identify adequate and superior work.

Many instructors use at least some of the following criteria:

1. Conscientiousness—willingness to work diligently at the journal.

2. Ability to distinguish trivial from significant statements.

3. Ability to use detail and develop ideas.

How often journals are collected and read depends on their purpose in the course. In my upper division courses, where the journal is used extensively, I usually collect them every two or three weeks. I skim all of the entries and request students to choose one entry for which they would like more extensive comments.

JOURNAL ASSIGNMENT

CRIMINAL JUSTICE 385: THEORIES OF DEVIANCE
Finn Hornum

Writing Assignments

Two written assignments must be completed: A Theory Journal and a Term Project. The latter will be written in several stages.

Theory Journal

Purposes: There are several purposes for keeping this journal:

+ To encourage you to react independently to the materials read and the class discussions.

+ To help you clarify your thinking about the readings before you come to class.

+ To help you evaluate and revise your initial reactions after class discussions of the readings.

+ To help you develop a body of information that you can use when taking exams and when writing the required term paper.

Content

First, you should use the journal to record your initial reactions to the readings. Second, you should record corrections and additions *after* the material has been discussed in class.

Since the major objective of this course is to study the relationship between theory and practice, the following questions should be addressed for each "school" or theory covered:

With respect to the *theory* itself:

1. What is the theory's assumptions about the nature of human nature?

2. What is the theory's assumptions about the nature of society?

3. What is the theory's assumptions about the relationship between the individual and society?

4. What is the theory's propositions on the causes of deviance?

5. What are the major conceptual criticisms of the theory?

6. To what extent has the theory been the subject of empirical research and what has been the results of this research?

With respect to *practice:*

7. What criminal justice goals or objectives can be derived from the theoretical perspective? If the theory was to serve as the foundation for implementation of criminal justice policies, what would be the aims of those policies?

8. What examples, if any, are there of criminal justice policies that appear to rely upon this particular theoretical perspective?

9. If practice does not seem to have made use of the theory, what types of procedures and programs would be consistent with the theory and why have they not been tried?

10. What have been the results of policies, procedures, or programs implemented on the basis of the theory?

It should be possible for you to answer the first five questions based upon your readings in the text. Remember, however, that your initial answers may well be modified by class discussions and lectures. For the last five questions, you will need to do some independent work in the library. The instructor will provide suggestions regarding suitable reference sources and will also cover much of this material in class lectures.

Audience

The journal is written primarily for yourself, but keep in mind that I will read excerpts from your journal on several occasions and that you will be asked to swap entries with other students in class. The writing may be informal, but it must be legible and intelligible.

Format

The journal should be written on loose-leaf paper (easier for me to collect and for you to add materials). Write at least one page for each set of readings on a particular school or theory. Date and title each page. Double space so that you have room for additions/changes subsequent to class discussions.

Grading

The journal will not receive a letter grade, but will be judged acceptable or not (+ or -), and will influence the class participation percentage of your grade.

JOURNAL ASSIGNMENT

FINANCE 303: INTRODUCTION TO FINANCIAL MARKETS AND INSTITUTIONS
Kathleen S. McNichol

An important objective of your study in the Financial Markets and Institutions course is the ability to read about and understand developments occurring in the financial sector. Reading a financial newspaper keeps you informed of current events and reinforces many theories and concepts learned in class.

Your Finance Journal is a *bound* notebook (no spiral notebooks) in which you record your ideas, comments, evaluations, and questions pertaining to an article read each week from the *Wall Street Journal*.

The Finance Journal will be reviewed several times during the semester. I will read your Finance Journal to determine how well you understand the content of the article and attempt to track improvement during the semester. Entries will be marked "good," "fair," or "poor" depending on: (1) your ability to relate information to course content and (2) the logic and rationale with which you express your thoughts.

Each journal entry should be approximately 2–3 handwritten pages per article and consist of:

1. Entry date (the date you are writing the entry).

2. Title, date, and author of the article.

3. Short summary of the article.

4. Your reaction to the article.

5. Article clipped and *fastened* in your journal.

Topics of the articles can vary. However, I request that you read several articles concerning (a) ethical issues in the financial world and (b) international finance issues.

In formulating your reaction to each article, consider the following points.

1. How does the material in the text or in the class lectures help you to understand and interpret the article?

2. Can you use a theory or principle from the course to explain how or why the event developed as it did?

3. Can you use a theory or principle from the course to analyze the impact that the event presented in the articles has had or is having on lenders, borrowers, financial institutions, interest rates, or security prices?

4. Did the author present primarily fact or opinion? If opinions were expressed, use theories or principles from the course to determine whether you agree or disagree with them.

Late entries will not be accepted. Your final grade for the journal depends on the overall *quality* of the entries and the *number* of entries you submit.

Submission Dates

October 10	(3 entries)
November 13	(4 entries)
December 10	(3 entries)

JOURNAL ASSIGNMENT

SPANISH 302: ADVANCED CONVERSATION AND COMPOSITION
Glenn A. Morocco

Informal Writing in Spanish
Required Notebook and Supplementary Readings
Guidelines: WRITE IN SPANISH

Notebook activities for SPN 302 are augmented as indicated below.

You will write in your class notebook in *SPANISH*. NOTEBOOKS, especially portions on the supplementary readings, MUST BE INSPECTED BY DR. M. AS PART OF YOUR PARTICIPATION GRADE (1/3).

In addition to grammar exercises, notes for talks, drafts for compositions, and class notes, etc., you are to write at least one page in a standard size notebook for every reading assigned. For the first half of the semester the readings will be given to you in the form of photocopies. During the second half of the term, you are to go to the library or language lab to find an article in a Spanish language newspaper or magazine. Choose articles of at least one page in length whose subject is of general interest in the areas of politics, economics, sociology (life in today's world), etc. Do not pick articles of local interest only or those that are of the gossip-column variety.

You may write in the first person—"Yo creo que..."

Before beginning each entry, write on the top of the page the author, name of the article in "_____" quotation marks, *source* (what magazine or paper), and the date of the article. You are to do a little more than summarize.

Here are some guidelines:

- What does the author state?
- Does the author argue a point or relate a story?
- Are the arguments good? Consistent? What are they?
- Are the arguments supported by evidence?
- What is the bias/slant of the article (does the author take sides or is he/she impartial?)
- What did I learn? How has my view of this subject changed?

You do not have to answer all these questions. Are there other points you should cover? Did you include pertinent information?

THE PERSONAL-RESPONSE ESSAY

> "The liberal arts—if the words mean anything—must connote the preeminence of the freedom of the individual. And this freedom begins with the freedom of the individual to express his or her emotional and aspirational goals. . . .Yet our curriculum does not make explicit provision for self-expression."
>
> (James L. Kinneavy, *Thinkings* 180)

The Personal Essay Defined

As developed in the seventeenth century, and later revived in the nineteenth century, the personal essay is a carefully controlled self-exploration or a probing analysis of the self in relationship to events, other people (society), or the world. The author may conduct this analysis from the vantage point of the past, the present, or the future. For example, when writing about "the world" these questions might be addressed:

- Describe the physical, social, and political environments in which you have existed, and how they have affected you.

- Describe your standing now in your society and your physical environment. How are they helping or hindering you?

- What are your goals for using the physical, social, and political worlds to your best advantage, and your plan for getting there?

These same questions can be modified for self-exploration in relationship to events or an examination of the self in relation to others. (See Table 1, page 37.)

In the past, when students wrote personal essays in school, they wrote them in English classes, usually in composition courses. That is no longer the case, since the goal of most composition courses today is to prepare students for the kinds of writing they will be assigned in other college courses. The personal essay, a popular genre in the seventeenth and nineteenth century, and in our own time favored by such essayists as Annie Dillard, Loren Eiseley, Joan Didion, and Garrison Keillor, has all but disappeared from the college curriculum.

Yet, this personal writing can play an important role in the college curriculum by helping students understand how to use their courses to make sense of their own lives. Assignments that require self-exploration in relationship to events, other people, or the world can take several forms other than the essay. Journals and logs can become vehicles for students to record personal responses to experience or readings.

Admittedly, personal writing may be more appropriate in some courses than others, for example, foundation courses or courses like those in psychology where self-understanding is one of the primary objectives. In a psychology course entitled *Personality Dynamics and Adjustment* students write several personal essays, in addition to other kinds of writing (see sample assignments). Assignments in the science foundation courses ask students to examine the relationship between technology and their own lives. In a course entitled *Consumer Chemistry*, for example, students write about the personal impact of ecological events such as the disappearance of the ozone layer (see examples that follow).

The Organization and Style of the Personal Essay

The organization of a personal essay depends heavily on the essay's subject matter. If the essay is about an event, it will most likely be organized chronologically, interspersed with accounts of feelings and ideas along the way. For example, in response to an assignment that requires students to attend a worship service and reflect on how the service speaks to their needs, one student, addressing her essay to the Congregation of Germantown Friends, begins the discussion about the service this way:

> "For over a year I have been passing by your meeting house and saying to myself this Sunday I'll go. In fact Quaker friends of mine believed that I might find the service enlightening. Yet, until now I have for various reasons avoided the opportunities of attending meeting. On this cold winter's morning with the full meaning of war upon the nation and myself, I looked forward to being surrounded by people who also believed war to be wrong. Upon entering the house, two members of the congregation introduced themselves, . . ."

Elements typical of the style of the personal essay are illustrated in the excerpt from the student essay quoted above. The first person pronoun is perfectly admissible, as well as the expression of emotions. Language usually conveys more than just information. It helps to express the mood of the author, such as in the sentence beginning, "On this cold winter's morning . . ."

Assigning the Personal Essay

Perhaps the greatest obstacle in assigning the personal essay is student attitude. Students may have had some experience writing the personal essay in high school or in freshman composition where instructors may assign one or two such papers in the beginning of the semester. However, for the most part, their education has stressed the value of objectivity, underscored by the warning never to use the personal pronoun "I" in an essay. Therefore, class discussion about the purposes for personal writing is essential when assigning an essay or other form of writing that requires writing about oneself. Giving students a list of questions such as the checklist that follows can help them to focus their thinking. Unaccustomed to exploring their feelings and personal beliefs, they often need a heuristic for structuring their analysis.

Evaluating the Personal Essay

"Good ones [personal essays] enlighten the authors about themselves and, because people share many characteristics, they enlighten the readers as well" (Kinneavy, *Liberal Arts Tradition* 42). Furthermore, good personal essays convey a mood or tone. Acknowledging this accomplishment in a student paper, an instructor wrote: "Your description of what happened is personal and deeply touching." This checklist can be used both as a guide for writing and evaluating the personal essay but will need to be modified to suit the specific assignment.

The Personal Essay Checklist

1. Does the essay enlighten the reader through an interpretation of self, the self in relation to others, or the self in relation to the world?

2. Is there sufficient description of events and people?

3. Are there sufficient observations about the events or people?

4. Does the essay convey the author's moods or feelings?

5. Has the author responded to all the questions of the assignment?

6. Is the style personal? (Usually includes the personal pronoun, descriptive adjectives, conversational language)

7. Are mechanics correct?

CONNECTING LEARNING TO PERSONAL EXPERIENCE

BIOLOGY 156: HUMAN GENETICS
Bro. Thomas McPhillips, F.S.C.

WRITING ASSIGNMENT #2

For the second writing assignment for this course you will write a short paper on the topic of hemophilia. Introductory information on this topic is available in your textbook. In this paper you are to expand upon this discussion. Your paper should include a brief description of the condition (symptoms), a review of the genetics of the condition, possibilities for cure and/or treatment, and a prognosis for the affected individual. The discussion of these topics should be brief. (Make sure to reference any sources you use.)

The major part of the paper will be a discussion of how an individual affected with this condition might affect family life. Topics might include monetary effects, direct effects on normal siblings, and effects on future generations. You might consider any ethical questions that family members might have to deal with as a result of having an affected member. Primarily you should consider the personal and sociological implications of this genetic condition.

Length: The paper should be approximately three pages long.

Audience: Your audience will be a fellow student who has a basic knowledge of Mendelian genetics but no familiarity with the condition you are discussing. Therefore you must present necessary background information.

Draft: Before you submit the paper for grading, you will submit a typewritten draft for evaluation by our writing fellow, Joe Irwin. Joe will make comments on your writing but will NOT grade the paper. The paper will be graded only after the draft has been returned to you and you submit a final copy. Grading the paper will be done only by BTMcP.

Format: The paper and the draft are to be typewritten (or word processed) double-spaced on 8 $\frac{1}{2}$" x 11" paper. Include a title page with an appropriate title, your name, and the date.

Style: Use a formal writing style. Do not use contractions or abbreviations.

Grading: 55%   Clarity of presentation, organization, accuracy of information.

20%   Grammar, word usage (number agreement, parallel structure, clear pronoun references).

10%   Spelling/typographical accuracy.

5%   Neatness and format.

10%   Following directions (includes meeting deadlines and keeping of appointments with writing fellow); addressing assigned topics.

Schedule: Fri., Mar. 23—Submit first draft; sign up for consultation with writing fellow.

Mon., Mar. 26
   thru

Fri., Mar. 30—First draft returned to student during scheduled consultation with writing fellow.

Wed., Apr. 4—Submit final copy of paper (with first draft and "Comments" page stapled to final copy).

CONNECTING LEARNING TO PERSONAL EXPERIENCE

SPANISH 302: ADVANCED COMPOSITION AND CONVERSATION
Glenn A. Morocco

Job Application Letter

Composition #2, Instructions:

This is a three-part written assignment.

1. La-carta-ofrecimiento de servicios personales.

2. Expediente-personal (Curriculum Vitae).

3. Un parrafo breve sobre el tema siguiente: Lo que quisiera ser y como he llegado a tomar esta decision.

   (See photocopies in Spanish of model letters and CV.)

Items 1 & 2: Follow the models given to you on separate sheets.

Your assignment is to apply (solicitar) for a job in writing after seeing a newpaper advertisement. Prepare a letter and a CV. Address your letter to a specific person. You may invent that person's name and title and address if you wish. Be sure that you make your letter a declaration of your capabilities and qualifications. The models are guides and should be used for that very purpose.

Your audience is your future employer, and you want to express yourself to the best advantage.

Item 3: Is a personal statement that is indirectly related to the letter. It is a statement that you will present to the class. At the time of the reading of these statements, the rest of the class will listen, take notes, and then take a short quiz to evaluate how well you can express yourselves and understand what is said in class.

- Your statement should take about 1 to 2 minutes to read.

- Your composition (letter and CV) will be graded as follows:

    Content, organization, grammar.

(The above refer to your grasp of ideas and subject, how well you communicate, how well you present your thoughts in paragraphs, sentences, vocabulary, focus and direction, and how appropriate the work is for the audience.)

CONNECTING LEARNING TO PERSONAL EXPERIENCE

PSYCHOLOGY 205: PERSONALITY DYNAMICS AND ADJUSTMENT
Thomas N. McCarthy

Adaptive Behavior Journal

Select an aspect of your personal life that you would like to understand more fully and that you want to change for the better.

You are free to select any aspect of your life that you wish. Some examples include the way you study; your relationships with someone: a special friend, parents, a brother or sister, a supervisor on your job; your choice of major; your choice of career; your sexual feelings and behavior; getting along in a current job; drug or alcohol use; your health; the way you worship; etc.

During the two week period beginning February 27 and ending March 12, keep a daily journal describing your thinking, feelings, decisions, and behavior as they relate specifically to the aspect of your personal life that you choose to observe.

Set aside time toward the end of the day to write the journal. Keep a record of what thoughts you had, feelings that occurred, decisions you made, actions you took, outcomes of your actions. How helpful (or unhelpful) were your thoughts, feelings, decisions, actions? In what ways? Also keep a record of the circumstances of your daily life during this period. Where were you? With whom? How helpful (or unhelpful) were these circumstances and people?

At the end of the two weeks, write a short statement—three or four double spaced, typewritten pages—describing what you observed about yourself: look for patterns or themes, general and specific influences on you, the nature of those influences, for example, how important were personal characteristics, situational factors? Did you like what you learned about yourself? Specifically, what steps can you take to improve your adaptive competencies in this aspect of your life? Will you take those steps now? How? Give two or three examples of how your journal relates to what we are covering in the course.

Both the daily journal (may be handwritten) and the summary statement (typed) will be turned in. College-level writing is required.

Personal Effectiveness Goals: An Integrative Statement

Using the outline below, write a statement describing how you currently see your goals and your plans for achieving them in each of the four areas that we have been covering in the course: work, leisure, love, and worship.

There is no prescribed length for the paper. You might think in terms of four or five double-spaced typewritten pages.

(See Table 1, adapted from Kinneavy, *Liberal Arts Tradition* 37.)

TABLE 1

Personality Dynamics and Adjustment
Psychology 205-01

Spring term, 1991

Paper #4

Due: April 15

Personal Effectiveness Goals: An Integrative Statement

Using the outline below, write a statement describing how you currently see your goals and your plans for achieving them in each of the four areas that we have been covering in the course: work, leisure, love, and worship.

There is no prescribed length for the paper. You might think in terms of four or five double-spaced typewritten pages.

Outline of Integrative Consideration

	Past	Present	Future		Guidelines
			If you don't plan	Your plan or goals	
You and the self	What were your inherited and acquired characteristics?	What you are like now, in terms of your emotional self, your rational self, your spiritual and your physical abilities.	What you will probably be like in the future if you keep going in the present way.	Your goals for improving yourself, and how you plan to get there (based on a realistic assessment of what you are capable of becoming).	Your standards for judging your progress toward these goals.
You and others	Your past position in relation to others with whom you have come in contact. How you stood with them, how you were regarded.	How you stand in relation to the people around you. What they think of you.	How you will stand with others if you continue in the present way.	Your goals for your future standing with others, and how you plan to get there (based on a realisitic assessment of your chances).	Your standards for judging your progress toward these goals.
You and the world	The physical, social, religious, and political environments in which you have existed, and how they have affected you.	Your standing now in your society and your physical environments. How are they helping or hindering you?	How you will stand in relation to the society and your physical environment if you continue in the present way.	Your goals for using the physical, social, religious, and political worlds to your best advantage, and your plan for getting there (based on a realisitc view of the world).	Your standards for judging your progress toward these goals.

Adapted from "Outline of Expressive Considerations"—Kinneavy. Liberal Arts 37.

THE SUMMARY ESSAY

The Summary Defined

In a general sense, the summary is a restatement in the author's own words of the contents of a passage, a group of paragraphs, a chapter, an article, or a book. Writing summaries requires understanding the central idea of a document in order to determine the main points that compose it, perceiving the principle of organization that structures the document, being able to distinguish key examples, and recognizing the author's point of view. However, the form the summary eventually assumes is strongly influenced by the purpose and audience for which it is written and the complexity of the material being summarized. For example, for writing summaries in business, Harty and Keenan recommend usually eliminating the following:

- Background discussion
- Personal comments
- Digressions
- Conjectures
- Introductions
- Explanations
- Examples, especially lengthy ones
- Visuals
- Definitions, especially long or complicated ones
- Data supported by assertions, rather than evidence

(Harty and Keenan 222)

In contrast, summarizing an article for an audience less knowledgeable than one's peers will require including such evidence as definitions, but translating that evidence for the secondary audience.

The organization of the summary does not necessarily have to follow the organization of the original. For example, an executive summary of a report often includes the findings and recommendations in the introductory section.

An important characteristic of all summaries is their objectivity; the author omits injecting an opinion.

Summaries can be assigned for several purposes:

- To help students understand required readings.
- To help students understand readings that will be used as the basis for other papers, such as the review paper or the critique.
- To teach students how to refer to another writer's ideas in the course of making their own original statements.

◆ To teach students how to summarize documents for specific audiences

Some teachers ask students to summarize difficult readings. For example, to help students learn to read philosophy, Prof. Richard Strosser assigns summary writing in an introductory philosophy class. When students are forced to put the material in their own words they are more apt to understand it.

Alternately, summary assignments can be useful as stages in the process of writing a longer review paper. In this case, students who are unfamiliar with the secondary literature in a field can receive guided practice in reading that literature through summary writing.

In courses where students are learning to write for a variety of audiences, summary writing can help them to understand the needs of those audiences. In business courses, the executive summary that accompanies a report might be a typical assignment.

Assigning the Summary

The general principles of summary writing are often taught in freshman composition. Students write summaries of readings as part of the process of learning how to incorporate readings in their original essays.

However, because the contents of a summary are closely related to the style and format of the original document, instructors should review the special characteristics of the written materials in their discipline. Summarizing a philosophical essay requires attending to the shape of the argument, whereas condensing an account of an experimental study in psychology requires the ability to reduce each section without losing significant information. For example, the methods section of a report might be reproduced in its entirety.

These understandings can be made explicit by a trial run—a class exercise in summary writing that precedes the assignment. The instructor can demonstrate the information in the original that should be deleted, the information that should be emphasized, and the appropriate length. Models of sample summaries attached to the original document also help to illustrate the relationship between the two. Such a lesson serves more than the purpose of teaching the summary; through this process students are learning how to read the texts of the discipline.

Evaluating the Summary

The following checklist can be used as both a guide for writing the summary and a form for evaluation. It should be modified to suit the specific assignment.

Summary Checklist

1. Has the document been identified appropriately (title, author, publication information)?

2. Are the main ideas of the original document clearly stated?

3. Are the relationships between the main ideas clearly indicated?

4. Are important examples and explanations included?

5. Is all essential information (names, costs, places, dates, etc.) included?

6. Is the length of the summary appropriate, in view of the purpose of the summary and the complexity of the material?

7. Have you avoided injecting your own opinion or additional information?

8. Are mechanics correct?

SUMMARY ASSIGNMENT

ECONOMICS 302: MANAGERIAL ECONOMICS
H. David Robison

Reading Summaries

You are to write executive summaries of the four articles with ** next to the author's name. The due dates will be given in class. The summaries are to be no longer than ONE double-spaced typewritten page each. They should summarize the author's basic points, method, and/or attitudes. Naturally, spelling, grammar, typing accuracy, and clarity count as part of your grade. The summary should be written as though I have not, and will not, read the article. Additional and more detailed comments on the summaries are given on the following page.

This assignment, in part, results from a study originally done by Shell Oil Co. and replicated by a number of others. The Shell study tried to determine what characteristic(s) those who reached the top level of management in major companies had in comparison with similarly trained people who did not advance to top levels. The only systematic difference they found was that managers who rose to top levels had the ability to write "good" one-page memos. More specifically, top managers were more efficient at communicating—absorbing large amounts of information and boiling the info down to one page. The one page provided all the necessary information with no extraneous or useless information. The reading summaries are your chance to practice writing short, concise, information-packed essays or memos. In writing these summaries, you may notice that it is easier to write two to four pages than it is to write just one. However, as commonly put, "if you can't say it in a page, you don't know what you want to say."

I strongly recommend reading the McCloskey book to students who have difficulty in writing or are too wordy in their writing! McCloskey provides an excellent framework on how to approach and complete a business writing assignment.

Notes on ECON 302 Reading Summaries

Requirements

1. The summary must be no more than one page long.

2. The summary must be double-spaced and typed with reasonable margins.

3. Write the summary under the assumption that I have NOT and will NOT read the article.

Hints and other comments (in no particular order):

1. The articles are too long to present all the information contained in the article. Therefore you must decide what is the most important idea/concept being conveyed. I typically refer to this idea/concept as the focus of the article. Once you have decided what the focus of the article is, write the summary presenting that focus. In order to adequately present the focus, you may need to delete other portions of the article entirely. Unless your chosen focus is ridiculous for the assigned article, the grade will be determined by how well you present your chosen focus and NOT by whether I agree with your focus.

2. GET RIGHT TO THE POINT OF THE ARTICLE!!! Given the one-page limitation, you do not have time to write an introductory paragraph that gives some background information. I STRONGLY RECOMMEND THAT YOUR FIRST SENTENCE BE what you would say about the paper if you got only one sentence (get straight to the focus). The first paragraph might best be what you would say if you got only one paragraph. The rest of the paper should then support and explain your first paragraph. Avoid repetition of ideas.

3. You are writing a summary of the article; thus you do NOT need to, and should not, put a "summary paragraph" at the end of your summary.

4. I read the papers quite literally. BE precise in selecting your words. If you mean always, say always; if you mean generally, say generally; and if you mean sometimes, say sometimes.

5. Spelling, grammar, and typographical errors will lower your grade. Accurate PROOFREADING is critical. If you have problems with English grammar, find someone who will proofread your drafts.

6. I am willing to proofread a legible draft of your summaries on an "as time permits" basis. By "as time permits" I mean if I have time, I will read it. Obviously the earlier you submit the draft, the more likely it is that I will have time to read it.

7. To test whether your summary is understandable to someone who has not read the article, have someone who is business literate (at least somewhat) but has not read the article proofread it for you. If they can explain to you what the article was about, you have done your job.

8. Some words that frequently indicate that you are wasting space: "tells," "discusses," "explains," and "will show." Don't tell me that you are going to tell me X and then tell me X; just tell me X to begin with and save the space.

9. Because each summary deals with only one article, there is no reason to give footnotes when you take a direct quote. I will presume that all quotes are from the assigned reading.

10. Just summarize the articles; provide no evaluation or other comments in the summary. In class you are welcome to comment on the difficulty of the article or the author's lineage.

11. Write the summary as if I have not, and will not, read the article. Thus any words for which the author gives NONSTANDARD definitions must be defined in your summary.

THE CRITIQUE AND BOOK REVIEW ESSAY

The Critique Defined

One of the major goals of college instruction is to teach students to read and think critically. We urge our students not to accept every source as equally valid and equally useful, but to distinguish crtically among sources by evaluating them (Behrens and Rosen 30). Therefore, it is not surprising that the critical essay and the book review, one kind of critical essay, are two of the most common writing assignments in all disciplines.

To write a critique students must be able to both summarize (see section on summary) and evaluate a presentation. As in the case of other forms of writing, the nature of the document being evaluated and the purpose and audience for the evaluation will influence the form of the critique. Beyond a few items that usually appear in all critiques (the title and author of the document and publication information, when necessary), the content and organization of the critique will vary, though most critiques address one or more of these questions:

- Has the author accomplished her purpose?

- Do I agree with the author's ideas?

- Is the information useful?

To respond to the first question, *Has the author accomplished her purpose*? the writer needs to consider:

a. What does the author state?

b. What does the author imply? Assume?

c. Is the information accurate?

d. Is the argument valid (internally consistent, logical? Do the conclusions follow from the premises?

e. Is the argument reliable (supported by evidence, authors)?

f. Has the author interpreted the information fairly?

(adapted from Norma Kahn, *More Learning in Less Time* 60)

The second question, *Do I agree with the author's ideas*? can be approached by considering questions that help to compare the material to other texts, disciplinary knowledge, or personal experience, such as. . .

How does the material relate to the following:

- My own experience, opinion, or knowledge?
- Other sources (oral or written) on the subject, for example, the textbook?
- Other theories?

In the case of evaluating research reports, the methods for obtaining the data can also be evaluated.

The third question regarding applicability, *Is the information useful?* questions the appropriateness of the information for various audiences:

1. How does this add to collective knowledge in the field?
2. For whom might this have value?
3. How can this change me (my views, my interest in the subject)?

Though critiques exhibit a wide variety of forms and organization, the following outline is fairly typical:

Introduction

- Introduce the essay or book and the author.
- State the author's main argument and the points you intend to make about it.
- Include background information that helps to place the essay or book in context (e.g., an explanation of why the subject is of interest, a reference to possible controversy surrounding the text or the topic, a reference to the intended audience).

The Middle Section

- Summarize the main points of the essay or book. The summary and critique sections may be integrated, or the author's evaluation may appear after the summary.
- Discuss the criteria used for evaluating the text. These can include all or some of the questions about the quality of the presentation, the validity of the argument, or the applicability of the material.
- Evaluate how well the text has met the criteria.

Conclusion

- ◆ Try to conclude with a comment that ties together the issues raised in the review. Remind the reader of strengths and weaknesses of the text.

Style

Critiques show wide diversity in style. Critiques on the basis of personal experience may be written using the first person pronoun ("I feel this book has helped to prepare me emotionally for the struggles of the business world..."), whereas the more standard critique assigned in college courses requires an objective style. The reviewer's response is often indicated through word choice as well as direct statements (e.g., "This book provides a *comprehensive* discussion on teacher training"). However, in all cases, statements of value should be supported with appropriate evidence. Half of the essay is usually devoted to the critique. An overabundant summary is a common weakness of critique essays by novice writers.

Assigning the Critique or the Book Review

The critique is often taught in freshman composition. However, recognizing that students are very reluctant to assume the evaluative perspective, the elements of the critique should be reviewed in other courses. The instructor should identify the nature of the critique: will it be based on personal experience, presentation, or the usefulness of the information? Instructors should also identify the special criteria needed to critique documents in their discipline. For example, if a book review is assigned in a history class, students need to be aware of the criteria for evaluating history texts. Models of successful student critiques may be useful.

A Note on the Annotated Bibiliography

The annotated bibiliography, assigned as a stage in writing the research paper or independently, requires the same skills as the critique. However, because annotations are typically brief, models should be distributed.

Evaluating the Critique or Book Review

This checklist can be used as both a guide for writing the critique and a form for evaluation. It should be modified to suit the specific assignment.

Critique/Book Review Checklist

1. Has the document been identifed appropriately (title, author, publication information)?

2. Is the author's main argument and the points you intend to make about it stated clearly?

3. Is appropriate background information included?

4. Are the main points of the text summarized?

5. Are the criteria for the review explained?

6. Is the evaluation supported with sufficient evidence from the text? (Is the length of the critique section appropriate?)

7. Does the conclusion tie together the issues raised in the review?

8. Are mechanics correct (spelling, punctuation)?

CRITIQUE ASSIGNMENT

ENGLISH 108: COLLEGE WRITING II
Judith Trachtenberg

The Critique
Choose one of the following topics:

♦ Which essay in either of the units we've read best reflects your view of the topic?

♦ Write a review of *The Informed Argument*. Let your audience know how valuable and reliable a source the book is.

Process—Clarify your thoughts by answering:

1. What do you think is the author's main point? Purpose?
2. Is the purpose aimed at a specific audience?
3. What information or knowledge does the book convey?
4. What purpose or practical meaning does the piece hold for you?
5. What are the most appropriate terms by which to evaluate the piece?
6. How does material relate to
   a. your own experience?
   b. other sources?
7. What might improve the book/essay?
8. For whom might this piece have value?

Based on the criteria you have just chosen, how successful was the author in achieving the overall purpose?

Form of Critique

1. Introduction—Discuss piece and author. Thesis might tell your reaction to piece.
2. Body:
   ♦ Summary of piece.
   ♦ Special purposes and audiences.
   ♦ Your reaction and evaluation.
3. Conclusion—There are lots of things you can cover here. You may want to argue with specific points or discuss matters the piece has left out. You may want to explore a personal experience related to the subject.

CRITIQUE ASSIGNMENT

RMI 302: RISK MANAGEMENT
Kathleen S. McNichol

Article Review and Critique Project

Review three (3) recent articles related to any aspect of life insurance. A "recent" article is one that has been published any time since March, 1989 to the present. For each article,

1. Cite the Title, Author, Publication Source, Date, and Page Numbers.

2. Give a descriptive summary of the major points made.

3. Evaluate the content. To aid in critical reading, ask yourself:

   ◆ What does the author state?
   ◆ Are the arguments consistent?
   ◆ Are they supported by evidence?
   ◆ Do the arguments appear biased?
   ◆ Can I restate the author's arguments in my own words?

To aid in creative reading, ask yourself:

   ◆ How does this article relate to what I already know about the subject?
   ◆ What additional arguments would make the article more sound?
   ◆ How has this changed my views on this subject?
   ◆ Has this article stimulated me to read more on this subject?

This project represents 15% of your final grade. It is intended to develop your critical and creative thinking skills related to insurance. Additionally, the project is designed to help you understand and learn from current life insurance literature.

BOOK REVIEW

FIN/RMI 314: RISK MANAGEMENT
Kathleen S. McNichol

Book Review and Analysis

The Risk Management profession strives for professional achievement and growth in a variety of ways. Two such avenues include continuing education programs such as the Associate in Risk Management (ARM) and active participation in professional organizations such as the Risk and Insurance Management Society (RIMS). Additionally, there is a large volume of literature that can serve to focus an individual on excellence in performance.

Imagine you are a risk manager who consciously strives to do the best possible job for your firm. To facilitate your thinking in the area of risk management excellence, read *A Passion for Excellence* by Tom Peters and Nancy Austin. Then

1. Critically review and analyze this work;

   ♦ Evaluate ideas and principles presented.

2. Apply the principles espoused by Peters and Austin to the risk management profession.

   ♦ How can you improve your performance and the performance of your department?

We will periodically discuss some of the ideas and principles in class prior to the due date. Therefore, to benefit from these discussions, it is important to read the book at a steady pace.

Your book review is typed and double-spaced and due on Thursday, October 24. As usual, late papers are penalized.

BE CREATIVE!!!!

THE SHORT ANALYSIS ESSAY

> "This paper will consist of an *analysis* of possible causes of a particular behavior, using the strategy illustrated in class."
>
> (Psychology—David L. Oden)

> "A major objective in this course is to have you begin to think critically about some of the problems facing the insurance industry. Your semester project will require you to research a problem, *analyze* the alternatives, and make suggestions for solutions."
>
> (Risk Management—Kathleen S. McNichol)

The Short Analysis Essay Defined

Perhaps the most frequently assigned task in college writing assignments is "analysis." The short analytical paper on a specific text or problem seems to be central in all disciplines, and longer research papers and reports invariably include an analytical section. But what do instructors mean by "analysis?" Do students understand what they mean when they assign an analysis paper?

As these two assignments illustrate, the term "analysis" is often used to mean both "take apart" and "explain" or "interpret," a distinction that helps us to explain this kind of writing to students.

For example, James Kinneavy defines analysis as the breaking up of complex notions into their elements, through classification, by determining their common characteristics, and through division, starting with a common class and breaking it up into smaller classes. He defines "explaining" or "interpreting" as "the selection of the rules or principles by which evidence can be interpreted. These rules must be acceptable to all members of the writer's audience of reasonable, objective people to whom these logical arguments are presumed to be directed"(*Liberal Arts Tradition* 132). In *The Little Rhetoric and Handbook*, Edward Corbett similarly includes interpretation in his discussion of the literary analysis essay; he says analysis requires "asking what the work is about and how the work is put together." Interpretation asks "what does the work mean" (259).

Dr. Oden's assignment includes both analysis and interpretation. It asks students to describe elements of observable behavior (analysis) and then to "give an analysis of the origins of the behavior, using the conditioning principles (various reinforcement contingencies or conditioned stimuli that might be controlling the behavior) discussed in class." The conditioning principles are the principles of interpretation acceptable to the audience (to use Kinneavy's definition), in this case, an audience of psychologists.

Each discipline uses distinctive methods of analysis and interpretation that students are required to practice in analysis essays. But many of the writing strategies employed are similar, regardless of the discipline. The analysis section of an essay is descriptive and often will be judged on the accuracy and detailed development of the description. For example, to continue using Prof. Oden's assignment as an example, he says, "Describe the behavior objectively. That is, what should an independent observer look for to determine if you are describing the situation accurately?"

The interpretation section of analysis papers is usually in the form of a discussion that integrates the principles of interpretation and the evidence that has been cited in the analysis.

Organization and Style of Analysis Essays

Because the organization of analysis essays is fairly standardized, understanding the two basic patterns of organization, the inductive and deductive, is essential in learning how to write these papers. The inductive pattern, common to the report, states the problem, presents the evidence, and then the intepretation. In contrast, the deductive pattern, which is represented in the thesis-support essay, begins with a thesis (the main point of the interpretation) and proceeds by supporting various elements of the interpretation. The literary analysis often follows this scheme.

> *Other content features should also be made explicit. For example,*

- Should the introduction include a definition of terms?
- How much and what kinds of evidence are required to support the interpretation?

If a conclusion is required, should it include a summary of the major points, an application of the findings to a larger sample, or a recommendation?

The style of analytical essays is objective; the evidence and mutually accepted rules of interpretation are the basis of the essay. In addition the writer must pay special attention to transitions, which are critical in writing that "uses careful reasoning" (Kinneavy, *Liberal Arts Tradition* 155).

Assigning the Short Analysis Essay

Most of the essays taught in freshman composition involve analysis. Nevertheless, the major pitfall in assigning analytical essays is to assume that students can easily transfer analytical skills from one context to another. Often they do not recognize the similarities between analyzing the structure of an argument, analyzing a short story, and performing an analysis of a criminal justice system. On the other hand, they may try to superimpose an interpretive scheme for one discipline onto another or limit themselves to generic schemes such as cause/effect. Because the short analytic essay is such a common assignment, it offers a unique opportunity to underscore both the similarities and differences between disciplinary methods of analysis. The general principles of analysis discussed in this section can be reviewed and related to the specific kinds of analysis required in a particular course.

Evaluating the Short Analysis Essay

This list is not comprehensive, since analysis papers assume many forms. For example, the introduction and conclusion can include other material, such as background information.

The Short Analysis Essay Checklist

The Thesis-Support or Deductive Analysis Essay

1. Is the thesis clearly stated in the introduction?

2. Are important terms defined?

3. Are the rules of interpretation explicit?

4. Is the quantity of evidence sufficient?

5. Are successive steps in the paper easy to follow because relationships between ideas are explicit?

6. Does the conclusion include a summary of main points, a recommendation, or an application of findings to a larger sample?

7. Is the style objective?

8. Are mechanics correct?

(For inductive papers the evaluation guide is similar to the guide for the report.)

ANALYSIS ASSIGNMENT

PSYCHOLOGY 150: INTRODUCTION TO PSYCHOLOGY
David L. Oden

Paper Assignment

The paper will consist of an analysis of possible causes of a particular behavior, using the strategy illustrated in class. First, select a behavior that someone (with less appreciation for rigorous analysis than you have) might attribute to an internal attribute. The behavior can be your own or that of someone or some category of person you interact with frequently (friend, roommate, family member, professors, other person who drives on the trip to school, etc.).

Describe the behavior *objectively*. That is, what should an independent observer look for to determine if you are describing the situation accurately? Obviously, something like "My roommate is an obnoxious creep who aggravates me all the time" is not an adequate description, even if it is true. In this section, just describe the observable behavior. You can develop a microtheory of what might be going on inside the person's head in a later section.

Next, briefly indicate how the behavior might be "explained" by reference to some internal property (which is actually no explanation at all). Then, give an alternative analysis (or possibly a couple of alternative analyses) of the origins of the behavior, using the conditioning principles discussed in class. That is, what are the various reinforcement contingencies or conditioned stimuli that might be controlling the behavior? Do you have any supplemental evidence to back up these ideas, or are they just guesses?

Finally, indicate how your new analysis might lead you to react differently to the behavior than you would have based on your original, "internal property" explanation.

Format

Cover the above topics in at least three, and not more than five, pages. Submit two (2) copies of your paper. One copy will be retained in the Psychology Department files and the other will be returned to you. Papers must be typed, doubled-spaced, on 8 $1/2$" x 11" paper. Allow at least one-inch margins on all sides. Follow the standard rules governing organization of ideas, sentence structure, grammar, and punctuation.

Evaluation

The paper will be evaluated for inclusion of the topics mentioned above, organization and clarity of the discussion, and *attention to mechanics*. The paper will be graded as OUTSTANDING (5 points), ACCEPTABLE (3 points), or INCOMPLETE/INADEQUATE (0 points). Late papers will have one point subtracted for each class period overdue. The paper must be submitted in person, during a regular class period (i.e., no papers stuffed under the office door at midnight). Less-than-excellent papers may be rewritten and submitted for reevaluation.

The paper is due on February 27. Earlier submission is encouraged, especially since your second exam is scheduled for the same week.

ANALYSIS ASSIGNMENT

COMPUTER SCIENCE 356: PROGRAMMING LANGUAGES
Margaret McManus

Writing Assignment #1

RELEASED: week 4

DUE: DRAFT: class 1 of week 6

FINAL PAPER: class 3 of week 6

Purpose: The purpose of this assignment is to teach the student how to write an analysis and evaluation of his/her FORTRAN program using our guidelines for programming language design.

Content: Your paper should discuss three programming language design categories from the six we have discussed in class:

- Data structures
- Data control
- Operations
- Sequence control
- Storage management
- Syntax

The paper should analyze your FORTRAN program according to each of the three categories. Show how the main features of the design category are implemented by concrete examples from your program. You should also evaluate how effective the FORTRAN language is for each of these categories for solving your programming problem.

Audience: Assume that you are writing for second-year computer science students who are familiar with the PASCAL language, but not with the design categories or FORTRAN. Include a listing and sample run of your FORTRAN program.

Form: The final paper should be 2 to 3 typewritten pages, double-spaced, and free from grammar and spelling mistakes. Diagrams, such as the contents of the stack of activation record and data structures used, should be included.

Evaluations: The papers will be graded on clarity and completeness of analysis and effectiveness of evaluation.

ANALYSIS ASSIGNMENT

NURSING 404: PUBLIC HEALTH NURSING—THEORY AND PRACTICE
Nursing Department

Short Writing Assignment

Class Weight = 20%

The objective of this assignment is to integrate the knowledge gained from information in the assigned readings, your texts, your own experiences, class materials, and class dialogues.

Select one of the topics below and respond in no more than four (4) typewritten pages. APA format should be used with appropriate references to sources.

Evaluation of the paper is based on clarity, accuracy, and understanding of the concept of public health nursing and on the integration into your paper.

Topics

1. a) A scoliosis-screening clinic at junior high school.

    b) Making a home visit to the parents of a child with a high absenteeism rate.

    c) Bandaging a child injured on the playground and contacting the appropriate personnel and family.

    d) Planning a first aid course for teachers.

    Explain how each of the above activities exemplify community-focused nursing practice. Respond to each activity separately.

2. Group roles are in part defined by the collection of behaviors that the person judges to be appropriate for himself/herself and in part by the expectations of others within the group. Discuss essential public health nursing roles in the 1990's and beyond.

3. You have been asked to collect data about a community's health facilities, vital statistics, and values regarding health. Which method of data collection would you select for each type of data and why?

4. Students may identify an alternative topic for the short writing assignment; however, this topic is to be reviewed with faculty members prior to start of paper.

ANALYSIS ASSIGNMENT

ART 206: NINETEENTH CENTURY PAINTING
Beverly Marchant

Paper: Painting and novels are very different media, but they correlate especially well in the 19th century, for artists of all kinds found creative stimuli in daily life. After reading one of the novels (below), write a paper comparing the fictional work to three 19th century paintings. (You may select works by one or more artists, but similarity of either style or content will facilitate the process.)

The novel and paintings you select are documents whose subject matter (theme), content (interpretation), and form and style (interpretative vehicles) you will examine by comparing and contrasting (similarities and differences). To help put your topic in focus you should note, in either the introduction or conclusion, whether the theme(s) on which you concentrated reflects the general human condition (i.e., are relatively timeless) or was (were) triggered by specific historical events or trends. If there are clear causes, note them in order to situate your topic historically.

Novels from which to select:

♦ Honoré de Balzac, *The [Unknown] Masterpiece*

♦ Charles Dickens, *Pickwick Papers* or *Little Dorritt*

♦ Gustave Flaubert, *Madame Bovary* or *Sentimental Education*

♦ Thomas Hardy, *Tess of the d'Urbervilles*

♦ Victor Hugo, *The Hunchback of Notre-Dame*

♦ Henry James, *The Ambassadors*

Proposal: Statement of topic (theme, novel, and [tentative] choice of paintings), basic outline, and bibliography are due on (date). Novel must be read EARLY!!!

Paper: No paper will be accepted unless a proposal has been approved, nor will any paper be accepted after class ends on (date). Paper must follow MLA form and be approximately 10 typed, double-spaced pages.

ANALYSIS ASSIGNMENT

CRIMINAL JUSTICE 324: *POLICE—* ORGANIZATION AND FUNCTIONS
Laura A. Otten

GUIDELINES FOR CASE ANALYSIS AND ARTICLE ANNOTATIONS

Introduction

These guidelines identify and discuss the necessary elements to a complete assignment: one case analysis and two article annotations. **During the course of this semester, this assignment will be done three times, with three different cases to be analyzed and a total of six different articles to be annotated.**

Purpose

The purposes of this assignment are as follows:

- To try, in the only way possible, to let the student play the role of and identify with a law enforcement officer.

- To role-play (in writing) not in the context of fantasy but in the context of the actual restraints and work environment that face the officer.

- To use the information received through the required readings and class lectures to act, in the role-playing, in an intelligent and informed manner, a manner consistent with a "real" officer.

- To broaden the student's knowledge base by requiring additional reading in professional journals of material directly related to the case at hand.

Tasks

There are two seemingly separate yet really very interrelated tasks in this assignment: a case analysis and reading and annotating two articles.

Each time this assignment is to be done, you are to select one case from a subset of cases from Miller and Braswell's *Human Relations and Police Work*. The list of possible cases, arranged by set, are attached as the last page of these guidelines. Having selected your *one* case for analysis, you will do the following steps:

1. *Recommended, but not required:*   Read the introduction to the section in Miller and Braswell in which the case you selected appears; this will give you a context for understanding your case.

2. Select two articles from a professional journal (the articles can be in the same or different journals); the subject of the articles selected should relate in some manner to the case which you are going to analyze.

3. Read and annotate the two articles (see below for instructions on annotations).

4. Using knowledge gained from reading the two articles and from class readings and lectures, analyze the case (see below for instructions on case analysis).

Article Annotations

What is an annotation?   An annotation is two fold. It is a brief synopsis of the content of an article and a critique of the method (not the substance) of that article. Annotations are used by researchers (and others) to get a quick and general sense of the substance and perspective of a work to determine if the full work ought to be read. Keep this function in mind when writing an annotation.

An annotation differs from a summary. A summary *gives* the content of an article; an annotation simply *informs* about the content of an article. The critique in an annotation is *not* a forum for rebutting the article's author, but rather a way of communicating to the reader of the annotation the article's particular strengths, weaknesses, and atypicalities in the approach to the subject matter.

What is the form of an annotation?   Each annotation should begin with a correct and complete citation of the article being annotated. *Rely on some discipline's standard bibliographic format; if you do not know one, ask.* After each citation, give your summary and critique.

Annotations should be typed and single-spaced, with double spacing between paragraphs. In general, there is *no* reason why an annotation should be longer than 250 words.

Case analysis

What is a case analysis?   A case analysis is a dissecting of a situation whereby you identify the questions or issues or problems raised in the case scenario and offer, for this assignment, *one* answer or resolution. Remember that the answer or resolution must be one that reflects the reality of law enforcement, taking into account the unique life and demands of the law enforcement subculture, legal restraints, and public controversy. Knowledge gained from class readings and lectures and the articles read for annotation should guide you in your analysis and support you in your resolution.

What is the form of a case analysis? While there is no set format for a case analysis, the following is offered as a model:

a. Introductory statement of the problem presented by the case.

b. Discussion of the questions or issues that the case raises (N.B.: The questions asked by Miller and Braswell at the end of each case should be used only as a guide; they are by no means comprehensive or necessarily good, nor should they replace your work.)

c. Discussions of the concerns or factors or ideas that will need to be considered in resolving the case.

d. The solution—the specific application of the ideas to the problem.

e. Implications of your solution.

f. Summary (if still necessary after "e").

The case analysis should be typed, double-spaced, and properly documented.

Audience

You are writing for an audience that has a lay knowledge of law enforcement, a knowledge based solely on personal experience and the media.

Grading

The assignment will be judged on content, substantiation, documentation, clarity, organization and logic, and writing.

NO LATE PAPERS WILL BE ACCEPTED.

THE ARGUMENT ESSAY

Resolved: "That the U.S. energy policy should mandate reduced dependence on oil."

In an essay not to exceed five pages, argue for or against this resolution. Do not equivocate: take a stand. Present a factually compelling and persuasive argument.

The Argument Defined

In this scientific age, informing and explaining have enjoyed far more prestige in the academy than argumentation. But argumentative writing is beginning to make a comeback, as colleges become increasingly concerned about preparing students for citizenship. Practicing the strategies of argumentation is excellent preparation for participation in public life. Similar to exploratory writing, argumentative writing is especially suitable for encouraging students to engage in active thinking and dialogue about social, political, and ethical issues.

The commonly accepted definition of argumentation is "that form of discourse in which the writer attempts to persuade an audience to adopt a certain position and/or to act in a certain way" (Corbett 20). How then, does argumentation differ from the analysis essay, which proves a point? Although the author of an analysis essay tries to convince the reader that her interpretation is correct, the primary aim of the analysis essay is expository—"to inform and explain" through an objective reporting of the pertinent evidence. While both forms rely on evidence, argumentation in the classical tradition permits the writer to depart from "strict scientific procedures" to select the kind and amount of evidence best suited to convince the audience.

Also, argumentation may rely on other kinds of appeal besides logical appeal, such as the appeal to the emotional needs of the audience and the appeal based on the "ethos or character of the speaker or writer" (Kinneavy, *Liberal Arts Tradition* 58). Politicians often rely on both. Instructors may want to point out how appeals based on emotion and ethos are used in their disciplines to strengthen arguments based primarily on logical appeals. To make this point, James Kinneavy requires students to write a persuasive essay on the same subject as a previous research paper, "using all the weapons of persuasion, including the credibility appeal of the author, the appeal to the interests and biases of the audience, and, of course, the logical arguments which the research has unearthed" (Kinneavy, "The Liberal Arts and the Current. . ." 17).

The organization of the argumentative essay follows the classical rhetorical pattern for an argumentative speech:

- The Introduction
- The Statement of the Issue
- The Proof of the Case
- The Refutation of the Opposing Case
- The Conclusion

The "Refutation of the Opposing Case" section, in which the author tries to attack opposing arguments, is not always included.

In argumentative essays based primarily on appeals to logic, the language will be objective. Repetition is commonly used as a persuasive tactic.

Assigning the Argument

Because argument is heavily influenced by audience considerations, instructors who assign persuasive essays should spend some class time on the expectation or needs of the audience. Students are unaccustomed to considering the audience's needs except in a general way. Once a special audience, such as the general public or the manager of a company, is specified, the characteristics of that audience should be reviewed.

The most difficult aspect of writing arguments for students is the discussion about the part of the argument that Stephen Toulmin, a language theorist and philosopher, describes as the "warrant." In Toulmin's model, arguments consist of claims, the assertions to be proven, data, information supplied as evidence to support the claim, and the warrant, the component of the argument that provides the abstract leap from the data to the claim. Toulmin gives this example:

- *Harry was born in Bermuda. (Data)*
- *Harry is a British Subject. (Claim)*
- *A man born in Bermuda will generally be a British subject. (Warrant)*

(Toulmin 102)

Warrants are equivalent to the "rules acceptable to all members of the writer's audience." Often the warrant remains unstated in professional argumentation. However, especially in essays where students are asked to make choices, stating the warrant may help them to be more precise. For example, if an assignment in a history class required students to argue that Jefferson had greater influence on the growth of democracy than other political figures, students might cite as evidence his authoring of the Declaration of Independence. In that case the "warrant" would be the significance of the Declaration of Independence in promoting democracy.

Preparation to write arguments might include some sample "Claim-Data-Warrant" exercises specific to the discipline as well as other strategies for introducing assignments discussed in previous chapters.

Evaluating the Argument

This list is a guide for arguments that rely primarily on the appeal of logic, but it includes some attention to the appeal of emotion and ethos—the author's character. However, most arguments will rarely include all of these sections. The checklist needs to be revised to suit the specific assignment.

The Argument Checklist

1. Does the introduction include:
   a. The claim to be argued?
   b. Definition of key terms if they are unfamiliar to the audience?
   c. The author's credentials?

2. Does the proof of the argument include a clear statement of the supporting claims and sufficient evidence?

3. Does the refutation include a statement of the opposing arguments and evidence to support their refutation?

4. Is the warrant clear?

5. Does the conclusion include:
   a. A summary of the supporting claims?
   b. An emphasis on the importance of the subject?

6. Is the style for the most part objective?

7. Are mechanics correct?

PERSUASIVE PAPER ASSIGNMENT

ECOLOGY AND ENVIRONMENTAL ISSUES
Bro. Craig Franz, F.S.C.

Does the Montreal Ozone Agreement Signal a New Era of International Environmental Statesmanship?

In 1974, a short paper was published in *Nature*, by M.J. Molina and F.S. Rowland, based on laboratory experiments, that warned of a potential threat to the stratospheric ozone layer resulting from the rapidly expanding use and release of a family of synthetic chemicals. This speculative prediction gave rise to an immediate controversy among the scientific, environmental, and industrial communities because of the essential role played by atmospheric ozone in shielding humans, as well as other terrestrial fauna and flora, from the harmful effects of the high-energy ultraviolet radiation emitted by the sun.

This problem is of global dimension and requires a concerted international response. Until recently, the only regulatory action was the banning of CFC pressurizers in spray cans (the least essential use of the chemicals) by the United States, Canada, and Scandinavia during 1976. Beginning in 1985, stimulated by the dramatic Antarctic findings, a series of yearly conferences have been held that culminated in a landmark agreement reached in 1987 in Montreal.

Does the Montreal ozone agreement signal a new era of international environmental statesmanship?

For your first writing assignment, do the following:

1. In an essay not to exceed four pages, prepare an answer to the question posed at the top of this page. Do not equivocate: take a stand. Present a factual, compelling, and persuasive argument. To assist you in preparing your argument, two informed responses on this issue are on reserve in the library for this course:

    YES: Mostafa K. Tolba. 1987. "The Ozone Agreement—and Beyond," *Environmental Conservation*. United Nations environmental executive Mostafa Tolba hails the recent agreement reached in Montreal on reducing the consumption of ozone-depleting chemicals as an indicator that other worldwide problems, such as global warming, will be approached in a similar manner.

    NO: John Gliedman. 1987. "The Ozone Follies—Is the pact too little, too late?" *The Nation* science writer John Gliedman, while acknowledging the significance of the Montreal pact, does not see signs that the "business as usual" approach to environmental problems is ending.

2. Papers must be typed with 1" left and right margins, 1.5" top and bottom margins. A cover sheet should be attached. Do not right justify.

3. Grading of this assignment will be based on writing style, rhetoric, and grammar (approximately 50%) as well as informational content (50%). The successful meeting of Writing Fellow responsibilities will also be computed in your grade.

4. On a final (fifth) page, list your references in full.

5. Please note deadlines:

   Oct. 3—First draft typed and submitted to writing fellow.
   Oct. 12—Final copy (and writing fellow's copy with suggestions) due.

   ## LATE ASSIGNMENTS WILL NOT BE ACCEPTED.

PERSUASIVE PAPER ASSIGNMENT

BIOLOGY 154 ECOLOGY / ENVIRONMENTAL SCIENCE
Bro. Craig Franz, F.S.C.

"Barge collision spills oil into Delaware River."
"Ozone levels exceed highest in recorded history."
"Philadelphia buried under waste disposal dilemma."

These headlines, and many more like them, have appeared in local newspapers during the past several months. Indeed, it is rare that one can read a daily news publication without seeing a story on an ecological or environmental science issue that merits attention.

In class, we have been sensitized to a number of issues that demand the attention of government agencies, local legislators, and state politicians. How often have we just read these stories and referred action to others while we do little ourselves to help correct the situation? There are many ways to assist in solving some of the problems that threaten our ecosystems and pose health hazards to our citizens. One way to take action is to express your environmental concern to people who can make a difference. Legislators, directors of environmental agencies, public statesmen—they all need to know the desires of their constituencies and one of the best ways to inform them is by letter.

As simplistic as that sounds, business letters are powerful tools in effecting change. (We all know what is mightier than the sword.) This assignment will allow you to do something that you have probably been wanting to do for a while but may not have taken the time to pursue—the writing of an environmental concern letter.

The Assignment

1. Select a topic of personal environmental concern from the *Philadelphia Inquirer* or the *New York Times*. Xerox or cut out this article together with the dated paper title and attach it to your final report. The article must be dated between Sept. 15, 1989 and Oct. 30, 1989.

2. Research this topic. What are the facts about the situation? What would you suggest be done to correct the problem? Prepare a two-page, single-spaced "fact sheet" summarizing your research (see attached).

3. Draft a letter to someone who is in a position to make the changes you desire. (It makes little sense writing to the Mayor about air pollution controls that are regulated by the Environmental Protection Agency. Write to the EPA Director for Air Monitoring & Quality, Philadelphia Division.)

4. Write a letter that (a) introduces yourself, (b) states your concern, and (c) suggests actions which that person can help implement.

5. Guidelines for the letter:

   - Utilize standard business format (margins, etc.)
   - Type the letter on 8 $\frac{1}{2}$" x 11" paper.
   - Single space the letter with proper spacing between the paragraphs, the salutation, complementary close, etc.
   - Type an envelope to accompany the letter, addressed correctly with your return address in the proper location.

6. The following should be paper *clipped*—not stapled—and returned in the following order:

   a. The original newspaper article with dated paper title.

   b. Your two-page typed "fact sheet" showing background information on the topic.

   c. The original letter signed.

   d. A copy of that letter (xerox acceptable).

   e. A correctly addressed envelope (stamp not necessary).

   f. The attached sheet showing references.

   g. Note the following dates:

      Oct. 31—Fact sheet and letter due to writing fellow.
      Nov. 5—Writing fellow interviews begin.
      Nov. 16—Final copy of all materials due today (no extensions).

THE EXPLORATORY ESSAY

The Exploratory Essay Defined

Most writing in high school and college is expository. From seventh grade on, the thesis-support essay is the focus of writing instruction. The library or research paper, as it is currently taught, is also expository. Students assemble information from texts to solve a problem, answer a question, and finally prove a point. However, educators on both the high school and college level are beginning to question this approach. They argue that while the ability to defend an assertion is a crucial skill, students should also be taught other forms of writing, such as the exploratory and persuasive essay. These essay forms are important for students to master because they require alternatives to deductive thinking that are often more appropriate for examining certain kinds of issues.

For example, moral, political, and social questions often do not lend themselves to an expository treatment. The difficulty of reaching closure about such questions requires another kind of thinking and writing described as "exploratory." Also, in some disciplines, for example, literature and philosophy, exploratory thinking and writing is an accepted mode for advancing new interpetations and theories. In these disciplines, assignments are apt to have exploratory features.

Exploratory writing and thinking are not new. Exploration was one of the several types of discourse distinguished by Aristotle. Demonstration aims at certitude. By contrast, Aristotle conceived of dialectic as distinguished from demonstration because its aim is not certitude, not yes or no, but probable truth. Dialectical thinking always concludes with qualified assertions; it is relational. It is the truth of something compared with something else. James Kinneavy, a contemporary rhetoritician, is credited with developing the classification "exploratory writing" based on his analysis of modern writings characterized by dialectical patterns. Kinneavy has argued that exploratory thinking and writing have been neglected because in the modern scientific era the prestige of demonstration, of proof, has made dialectical, or exploratory, discussion appear soft and less legitimate. He urges college educators to reverse this trend.

(Kinneavy, "The Liberal Arts and the Current. . ." 14)

The Organization and Style of Exploratory Essays

A comprehensive exploration of a subject requires raising a question about an accepted dogma or belief and searching for a new answer. In discussing the organization of exploratory writing, Kinneavy says that, "In contrast to other types of writing for which organizational patterns are specified by tradition, or editors, written exploration has no recommended pattern." This is partly because "many explorations are incomplete, being picked up in the middle of things . . ." and also because the writer has the prerogative to "search for the new answer" in her own way, sometimes following a narrative pattern as in Kinneavy's example of Thor Heyerdahl's *Kon-Tiki* (*Liberal Arts Tradition* 195). Many explorations, for example, use comparison as the major form of investigation.

The style of exploratory discourse is characterized by the same objective, denotative language found in expository papers, but exploratory writing often sounds more personal because words such as "it seems" and "perhaps" are used to remind the reader that the author is often suggesting a proposal, not proving a thesis.

Assigning Exploratory Writing

If instructors want students to write exploratory papers, then they must be explicit about the requirements for such assignments and be prepared to use class time for related instruction. Exploratory writing is not usually a part of the standard curriculum in freshman composition. Our students, accustomed to writing demonstrative papers, need considerable help in learning how to organize an exploratory discussion. In a Criminal Justice course, where two exploratory papers are assigned, students wrote better papers for the second assignment, which included more class preparation. Although the first paper was intended as exploratory, many students mistakenly wrote thesis-support papers.

(Criminal Justice Course) Assignment #1
What is Progress? The basic content of this paper should be to explore different definitions of the concept of progress based on readings and any additional library research you may find necessary. An exploratory paper on this subject should conclude with a hypothetical definition of progress; instead, students concluded with definitive sounding statements.

Evaluating Exploratory Writing

Exploratory writing should be evaluated on its own terms. Has the student successfully accomplished the strategies of an exploratory discussion? This checklist is for an assignment requiring a comprehensive exploration. Because exploratory writing has no recommended pattern of organization, the checklist does not include descriptions of the introduction and conclusion. This checklist can be used as a guide for evaluating exploratory writing but will need to be modified to suit the specific assignment.

The Exploratory Writing Checklist

1. Does the essay include an explanation of the issue or belief in question?

2. Is the evidence (facts, opinions) for questioning the belief explained sufficiently?

3. Have other attempts to answer the question been explained and compared?

4. Does the essay suggest a new belief that needs to be tested?

5. Is the language objective, but tentative?

6. Are mechanics correct?

EXPLORATORY PAPER ASSIGNMENT

CRJ 222: INTRODUCTION TO CRIMINAL JUSTICE
Finn Hornum

Guidelines for First Written Assignment

Background: In advance of writing this paper, you were recently assigned—and had the opportunity to discuss—two sets of readings dealing with the issues of "order" and "justice." The first reading was an excerpt from a book by Herbert Packer presenting the "crime control" and "due process" models of the criminal justice process. Packer contends that these models are based upon basic values and ideologies in American society. The second set of readings included selections from Sophocles' drama, *Antigone*, Thomas Hobbes' *Leviathan*, and John Locke's *Second Treatise on Civil Government*. These readings present some literary and philosophical views on the same basic value issues.

Purpose: The major purpose of this assignment is to explore and evaluate the moral/ethical propositions suggested by the Packer models, a tool for a social science analysis of the criminal justice process, in the light of the literary and philosophical readings.

Content: Your paper should be organized around the following questions:

1. What are the basic moral values represented in the Packer models? What are Packer's conclusions about the impact of these values on criminal justice policy?

2. What are the basic moral values dealt with in the Sophocles, Hobbes, and Locke readings? What positions do these classic writers take with respect to these moral issues?

3. How do the "classic" issues compare and contrast with those suggested in the Packer reading?

Format: The paper should not be more than 4–5 pages in length. It should be typed, double-spaced, and proofread before you turn it in. If you quote directly from the readings, you must include a proper citation.

EXPLORATORY PAPER ASSIGNMENT

CRJ 385: THEORIES OF DEVIANCE
Finn Hornum

Term Project

The written term project in this course is a very significant requirement. The two written papers will offer you the opportunity to write exploratory essays in criminal justice theory. Theoretical papers differ, on the one hand, from the usual term paper where the writer summarizes library sources and proceeds to draw conclusions regarding the relative merits of a particular program or practice and, on the other hand, from the traditional research paper in the social sciences where data are marshalled to prove a specific point. Rather, theoretical papers compare and contrast ideas and explore their logical soundness and implications, thus attempting to enlighten the reader rather than coming to a final closure.

The central concept in this course is the term "deviance." Throughout the course we will be exploring the ways in which different criminologists define deviance and speculate on its causes. There is a basic assumption that the particular view of deviance held by a theorist shapes the explanation proposed and the policies designed to control it. Thus, your first task is as follows:

- To write a short paper (4–5 pages) on "What is Deviance?" The basic content of this paper should be to explore different definitions of the concept of deviance based upon previous readings in criminal justice that you have done and any additional library research you may find necessary. This paper is due *Wednesday, Oct. 10.* After this paper has been graded and discussed in class, you should begin the second assignment.

- To write a second paper (10–12 pages) exploring the explication of a particular view of deviance in criminal justice theory and practice. This will involve the following tasks:

  1. Select a criminal justice program (past or current) described and evaluated in criminal justice literature.

  2. Prepare an annotated bibliography on your topic.

  3. From the theoretical frameworks covered in the course, select an explanation of the causes of deviance on which your criminal justice program appears to be based.

4. Write the first draft of your paper, including the following materials:

   a. A description of the selected criminal justice program

   b. A discussion of the theoretical foundation of the program

   c. An exploratory discussion of this program, based upon a comparison with other theoretical frameworks discussed in the course.

   The first draft of your paper is due Wednesday, Nov. 21. The first draft may be handwritten and use cut-and-paste techniques, but it should be sufficiently legible to be evaluated by the instructor.

5. Revise your first draft and write the final copy of your paper. Be sure it is typed, is double-spaced, and contains proper documentation. The final paper is due *Monday, December 10.*

You are not on your own with this paper. Each student will meet with the instructor for an initial discussion of topic selection and for additional conferences if you run into difficulties.

THE RESEARCH PAPER AND REVIEW ESSAY

The Research Paper and the Review Paper Defined

The research paper is an original essay presenting the student's ideas about information found in library sources. The student gathers material and gradually makes informed judgements and original interpretations. In contrast, a Review Paper is limited to a synthesis of references without original interpretation. In this case students trace patterns of thought in the literature, thereby showing the relationship between various works. For example, the first assignment in the Biology Department's senior writing component is a review paper:

> "The first writing project will be a scientific library review paper synthesizing contemporary references on an approved topic.... This paper will be substantive, rather than voluminous. Organizationally the paper will consist of the following sequence: introduction, body, summary, and references."

To write a research paper or a review paper the ability to **summarize** and **critique** individual sources is necessary, but not sufficient. In addition, students must know how to synthesize material from several or more sources, not an easy task for many students.

Instructors assign research or review papers for one or more of the following objectives:

- To teach students how to use the library.
- To teach students how to read the primary and secondary documents in the field.
- To give students the opportunity to pursue independently a subject of interest related to the course material.
- To teach students how to pose problems and solve them using methods appropriate to the discipline.

The form, structure, and style of these papers often reflects the conventions of professional writing in the discipline and the nature of the subject matter. For example, note the differences in the introductions of two review papers, one in Literature and one in Biology:

> Perhaps the most obviously strange aspect of Edgar Allan Poe's "The Fall of the House of Usher" is the setting. The bleak landscape, dim tarn, crumbling mansion, and miasmic atmosphere are nightmarish and inexplicable. They defy norms. But equally strange is Roderick's behavior toward his sister.

> The critical interpretations of the story are often as bizarre as the story. They range from incest, to vampirism, to madness.
>
> (Griffith 131)

> Most lamellibranch bivalves are sedentary, living either in soft-substrate burrows. . . or attached to hard substrate. . . . I will explore the morphological and physiological adaptations that make swimming possible in *P. maximus* and will consider some of the evolutionary pressures that might have selected for these adaptations.
>
> (Pechenik 103–104)

In the literature review paper the author rarely announces her intentions, whereas Pechenik says about Biology review papers, "The first paragraph of your paper must state clearly what you are setting out to accomplish and why" (106).

Documentation conventions are also dependent on the field. For example, because scientific essays are heavily referenced, the biology assignment advises: "Between 20 and 30 references are expected, of which approximately 75% are to be derived from primary sources."

Assigning the Research Paper

Library assignments, which teach the general skills needed for library work, such as locating sources, taking notes, and using proper documentation, are usually an important requirement in the freshman composition curriculum. The English Department often works closely with the library staff to coordinate library instruction with the assignments. As part of that instruction, students may receive an introduction to library sources. However, the noncomposition instructor should explain discipline-related conventions about form and content.

The first task the noncomposition teacher faces when planning a library assignment is to choose the kind of assignment most suitable for the course. The comprehensive research paper is often not the most effective one, especially in introductory courses. Many instructors believe that "most freshman and sophomores are singularly unprepared for this undertaking" (Kloss 30). When students are novices in a field, they are often ill equipped to develop a problem and a research plan for solving it. Some faculty believe that even in upper division courses the conventional research paper is not the best assignment. The review paper on a topic related to the course may be more appropriate, though shorter assignments such as journal articles, critiques, annotated bibliographies, pathfinders, or structured, limited research problems may be even more useful in some courses.

However, instructors who do assign research papers should keep in mind that assignments which offer the most choice are usually more difficult than structured research problems such as the following:

> "Deforestation has long been associated with human activities. Presently very severe deforestation is taking place in certain tropical areas. Where are these areas? What are some of the global consequences? Pick a particular area and describe the local effects. Consult the following sources for information: (sources provided)."
>
> (Earlham College Materials, 1991).

For longer, unstructured review paper assignments, guides that remind students of the issues that need to be considered are usually helpful. In the case of the senior project in Biology, the faculty chose to conduct a workshop for all seniors to discuss the process of writing a scientific review paper, including how to select a topic, choose sources, take notes, outline, draft, and edit. After conducting their research, students submit an outline for faculty approval. In general, it is good practice to give students feedback during the lengthy process of writing a research or review paper.

A Note about Synthesis

All too often library papers are list-like summaries of the sources the student investigated. Students have difficulty synthesizing various sources that "appear to take on the same subject and to have similar purposes." If points of comparison are suggested, students may be more apt to structure their papers around integrating ideas (Bazerman 221).

Evaluating the Library Review Paper

This checklist can be used as a guide for writing and evaluating the review paper. It should be modified to suit the specific assignment and discipline.

The Library Review Paper Checklist

1. Is the quality of the data adequate?

2. Is the quantity of data adequate?

3. Does the introduction include appropriate background information and a statement either about the author's purpose or the author's main argument?

4. Is the organizing principle clear (cause/effect, classification, chronology, etc.)?

5. Are the main points supported with sufficient evidence?

6. Are the relationships between texts clear?

7. Does the conclusion include a restatement of the problem investigated and the author's major points ?

8. Is documentation correct?

9. Is the format correct (when special format requirements such as headings are appropriate)?

10. Are mechanics correct?

(Modified from an *Evaluation Guide for Review Papers* by Dr. Alice Hoersch, Geology Department)

Note: If an original interpretation is required, then the quality of the interpretation will be an important part of the evaluation.

REVIEW PAPER ASSIGNMENT

ENGLISH 322: CHAUCER AND HIS WORLD
Marjorie S. Allen

Purpose: This assignment is meant to introduce you to several perspectives in medieval literary criticism and to have you apply those perspectives to the interpretation of a text. It will teach you the following:

a. To locate secondary sources in medieval literary criticism and to have you apply those perspectives to the interpretation of a text.

b. To identify the several schools of such criticism.

c. To contrast and evaluate those schools.

d. To use them in the interpretation of a Chaucer text.

It will also prepare you to begin your second paper after midterm.

Topic: One of the most problematic of Chaucer's Canterbury Tales is "The Clerk's Tale," the story of patient Grisilde who is abused by her husband and who has promised "In werk ne thoght I nyl yow disobeye." Interpreted by some as an injunction to obedience in marriage, by others as an injunction to obey God, by yet others as a rejection of the world, this tale forces the modern reader to embrace a particular approach to medieval texts. Although this tale may do several things, it cannot do all of them. How do you interpret this tale, and in particular the issue of "obedience" at its center, in light of the several major and often contradictory critical approaches presently accepted by medieval literary criticism?

Procedure:

1. The following modern critics are known for their very specific approaches to medieval literary criticism. In the next weeks, locate and summarize criticism either in an article or a chapter of a book by each of them, noting the general principles by which each interprets medieval texts.

   a. D. W. Roberston, Jr., *A Preface to Chaucer*

   b. E. Talbot Donaldson, *Speaking of Chaucer*

   c. Donald Howard, *The Idea of the Canterbury Tales*

   d. C. S. Lewis, *The Allegory of Love*

    e. Jill Mann, *Chaucer and Medieval Estates Satire: The Literature of the Social Classes and the General Prologue*

    f. Sheila Delany, "Womanliness in the Man of Law's Tale" *Chaucer Review* 9 [1974] pp. 63–72

    g. Charles Muscatine, *Chaucer and the French Tradition: A Study in Style and Meaning*

2. Write brief inital reactions to these approaches—approximately a paragraph.

3. Group them in terms of similarity of approach. Which are primarily historical? Which rely most heavily on the text itself? Which are interested in genre? What specific differences do you find in these interpretations?

4. Decide how each might respond to "The Clerk's Tale" and the issue of obedience it presents.

Writing the Essay: This essay should be about five pages in length. It should be properly documented (*MLA Style Sheet*) and should include summaries, reactions, evaluation by comparison and contrast, and application to the text. The order and organizational pattern that you select is entirely up to you. However, it must include a thesis paragraph and a conclusion.

Time Frame: You should begin this assignment immediately. It will take you five weeks to complete. I will collect summaries and responses three weeks into the course; they will be returned to you with commentary. The working draft of the paper will be collected in week four. These drafts will be distributed in class at the end of that week. Final papers will be collected at the end of week five.

REVIEW PAPER ASSIGNMENT

SENIOR WRITING COMPONENT IN BIOLOGY
Bro. Craig Franz, F.S.C.

Overview

At La Salle University, the Biology Department senior writing component is designed to assist the professional growth of the student by

1. Developing and refining writing skills specific to the biological sciences.

2. Training the individual in the mechanics and methodology of scientific writing.;

3. Providing an opportunity for the advanced student to engage in library research of a well-defined topic under the guidance of a faculty preceptor.

Scheduling

The senior writing component will extend over the fall and spring semester of the senior year. During this time, the student will select a topic of biological interest, receive an assigned faculty preceptor, receive approval for his/her topic, and be instructed in the mechanics and methodologies of scientific writing. The successful completion of two writing projects will fulfill the senior writing component requirement. Typically, the first project will be submitted by early February; the second writing project will be submitted by the beginning of April.

Evaluation

A grade will be determined by the faculty preceptor after evaluating both of the student's projects. Timely submission of required components will be included in the evaluation. All students will receive a "no pass" or "pass" designation at the conclusion of the senior year. Because we are linking this course to BIO 408, students must receive a "pass" grade in their senior writing component for their final BIO 408 grade to be released.

Project Dimension

The senior writing component will consist of two separate submissions that have been prepared on word processing equipment:

1. The first writing project will be a scientific library research paper, synthesizing contemporary references on an approved topic. This paper is to be prepared for a readership audience comparable to that addressed by the scientific journals that serve as primary references for the project.

   This paper will be substantive rather than voluminous. Organizationally, the paper will consist of the following sequence: introduction, body, summary, and references. Excluding references, tables, and graphs, this paper will be 10–15 pages in length. Margins of 1" right and left, 1" top and bottom are appropriate. Between 20 and 30 references are expected, of which approximately 75% are to be derived from primary sources.

2. The second writing project will be a paper that makes available to the common reader the content of the first paper, i.e., it will be written in a colloquial (nonscientific) style. This paper is to be prepared for a readership audience comparable to that addressed by the *Science Times* section of the *New York Times* or *Scientific American* (viz., an educated university student).

   This paper will present the major findings of the first project in a style comprehensible by the layman. Organizationally, the paper will consist of the following sequence: introduction, body, and summary. No references are anticipated. Excluding tables and graphs, this paper will be 5–8 pages in length. Margins of 1" right and left, 1" top and bottom are appropriate.

Deadlines

As the writing component proceeds, dates will be established for the submission of various aspects of the writing component. Late submission of the interest forms, topic, scope and outline, introduction and references, drafts and final copies will affect the final evaluation of your senior writing component.

THE REPORT

The Report Defined

The purpose of the report in both the business and academic community is to inform, though many reports include both analysis and recommendations. Depending on their emphasis, reports are classified broadly as informative or persuasive. In the persuasive report the author tries to move the reader to accept her conclusions and possibly to act upon them. Persuasive reports often suggest solutions to problems and/or propose policies.

Data for reports usually include firsthand observations of events, interviews, and primary written sources, such as other reports or records. One way of distinguishing between the report and the library-based research paper is to note that reports often remain closer to the context of the subject. For example, a "monthly report" is written on crime in Lower Merion Township, whereas an appropriate subject for a research paper might be the higher incidence of crime in cities compared to the suburbs.

The Organization and Style of Reports

The overall structure of reports in the social sciences, natural and physical sciences, and the business world is surprisingly similar. Reports usually include an introductory section that states the question the report is intended to answer. The problem statement is followed by a methods section describing the methods used to gather the information, a results section including an analysis of the findings, and a conclusion. Persuasive reports include a recommendation section. In almost all cases objective language is used to reinforce the validity of the conclusions. The format for the report is dictated by the discipline.

Assigning the Report

The report based on interviews and/or observations is sometimes an optional assignment in freshman composition. Some instructors at La Salle University routinely include it in their syllabus. For example, after reading Sissela Bok's essay "Truthfulness, Deceit, and Trust," students in Judy Trachtenberg's composition class write a report assessing the attitudes of their peers on the subject of lying.

Many students have had no experience writing reports, or, if they have written a report, they often assume that all reports are similar. When assigning reports, the noncomposition instructor should discuss the general principles of report writing and review the specific structure and format requirements of reports in his discipline. In some freshman composition courses basic primary research techniques, such as how to choose human subjects and how to develop interview questions, are part of instruction, but noncomposition instructors should assume that research techniques need to be taught if they are not an integral part of the the course content. For example, in *Writing Instruction: Theory and Practice*, a 300-level course taken by the Writing Fellows at La Salle University, students are taught how to gather and synthesize material for a Case Report, a kind of research report unfamiliar to most of them.

Students also need instruction in writing about findings. In some disciplines, such as the sciences, authors are encouraged to separate the raw results and statistical findings from a broader discussion of their implications.

As a way of organizing raw data, themes or major points of agreement can be used to develop a readable discussion. For example, if business people were interviewed to determine what attributes they look for in successful leaders, and most of them agreed that "a, b, and c" are essential attributes of effective leadership, the findings section should be organized around these points.

Students usually have the most difficulty writing the analysis or conclusion sections of reports, because these parts require considerable disciplinary knowledge. These sections answer the question: "What do the results mean?" Instructors may need to make explicit methods of interpreting data, or provide specific interpretive paradigms. For example, for the Case Report described above, students analyze evidence they have gathered about student writing problems using several theories concerning the causes of writing problems: poor attitude, lack of knowledge about the composing process, etc. Models of the findings and conclusion sections of reports are valuable aides for teaching students how to write these sections. (See section on Analysis Essays for more information.)

Evaluating the Report

This checklist can be used as a guide for writing and evaluating reports, but it should be modified to suit the specific assignment and discipline.

The Report Checklist

1. Is the quality of the data adequate?

2. Is the quantity of date adequate?

3. Does the introduction include
   - A statement of the problem?
   - Appropriate background information?
   - A statement of the author's purpose?
   - Definition of terms?

4. Does the methodology section include a detailed discussion of research methods (interviewees, questions, context, technical apparatus, processes, etc.)?

5. Is the findings section organized according to themes discovered in the data?

6. Is the discussion section, often called the "results" or the "conclusion," informed by appropriate theory or interpretive paradigms?

7. Is the language objective (no loaded words reflecting the writer's bias)?

8. Is the format correct (headings, etc.)?

9. Are mechanics correct?

REPORT ASSIGNMENT

GUIDELINES FOR LABORATORY REPORTS IN BIOLOGY
Annette O'Connor

All students are expected to submit formal written reports describing the laboratory exercises performed throughout the semester. These reports will be of importance in determining your final grade for the semester. The reports will be due one week after the completion of an exercise. Late reports will not be accepted. All reports must be on plain 8 $1/2$" by 11" paper. Ideally they will be typed. Any reports that are not legible will receive a zero. Spelling, grammar, and syntax will count in addition to the scholarship of the report's content.

Set forth below is a reasonably full outline of the manner in which many scientific reports are written. It is understood that exhaustive treatment is not expected. Quality counts more than quantity. **Be brief, but make your statements count.**

I. *Title*

The report should be prefaced with a title descriptive of the work actually done. Three spaces below the title put your name and the date. Also include the name of any partner who participated in the work and who will share the data obtained.

II. *Introduction*

This section must include an objective or objectives and pertinent background information.

An objective is a sentence or two stating in general terms the reason for doing the experiment, i.e., what you wish to demonstrate or learn. On numerous occasions the experiments you perform will be a series of related mini-experiments. In such situations you should introduce the main problem and then follow it with appropriate subordinate objectives.

The background information should include any information that clarifies your objective(s) or puts it (them) into proper perspective. Experiments of other workers that illuminate your experiment could be cited. Important concepts that the reader should bear in mind when reading your experiment could be included. Expected results could be mentioned, and so on.

III. *Methods and Materials*

Ordinarily, this section would specify the design of the experiment, the materials used, and the procedure followed; it would include information about the subjects (species, strain, histories, vital statistics, etc.), accuracy and reliability of the measuring instruments, sources of error that must be taken into account in interpreting the findings. All this information must be extremely clear—other scientists may wish to duplicate the experiment to check its validity and accuracy.

For most of our experiments much of the above information is provided in the laboratory instructions. Therefore, you may simply say, "refer to laboratory directions," or if you wish, you may include those directions as part of your report. Any modifications in the procedure introduced by you (or by the instructor) should be clearly noted.

In those instances in which you design the experiment you should write out a complete "Methods and Materials" section for it.

IV. *Results*

This section includes objective statements of what happened in the experiment *without* your evaluation. Whenever they lend themselves to this type of reporting, results should be neatly tabulated and/or graphically represented. Careful headings for tables and labels for graphic records should be briefly described in words; your description should make explicit the relationships between data shown in tables and graphs. For example, one might say that graph #1 shows that "as A increases, B decreases" or "as the stimulus increases from 0 to 20 volts the strength of the muscle contraction increases from 0 to 10 grams." Any unusual or unexpected occurrences should be mentioned and any notable omissions or deficiencies explained.

Usually the exercises you do will be concerned with more than one aspect of a particular problem, and in such cases it is desirable to subdivide the section on results under suitable subheadings.

V. *Discussion*

This is the interpretative segment of your report and is in many ways the most important part. It is here that you attempt to answer the question, "What do the results mean?" You should analyze the results and explain what lies behind them. Do not be satisfied with a superficial conclusion, but draw upon other sources of pertinent information (lecture notes, your text, reference materials) to construct a plausible explanation of the mechanisms that may underlie the observed findings.

Again, since you will often be concerned with more than one aspect of a particular problem, it may be necessary to subdivide this section like the section on results. Include a separate discussion section for each section of the results.

If by chance the experiment does not turn out as expected, which may happen on occasion for one reason or another, record the actual data obtained in the results section. Then in the discussion section explain that you think the data is incorrect. Follow this with a description of the expected results and account for them. Give possible reasons for the failure.

VI. *Literature Cited (or References)*

In writing your report, you may wish to refer to the published work of others in both the introduction and discussion sections. When doing so, refer to the investigator(s) by last name only, with the date of publication in parentheses and then, at the end of your report in the literature cited section (not as a footnote) list, in alphabetical order by author, the name of the author(s), date of publication, title of the article, the journal in which the article was published, volume number, and page numbers, in that order.

For example, the following is quoted from a lab report: "In his excellent review of the subject, Deevey (1947) summarized information up to that time and gives the method of computation for life tables."

In the literature cited section of the same report the following was given:

Deevey, E.S. 1947. Life tables for natural populations of animals. Wart. Rev. Biol. 22:283–314.

References from books are cited as follows:

Allee, W.C. et.al. 1949. *Principles of Animal Ecology*. W.B. Saunders Company, Philadelphia, PA.

THE ESSAY EXAM

"Two problems cloud the understanding of essay questions: teachers often do not make clear what is called for, and even when they do, students do not attend carefully to the demands of the question." (White 5)

Edward M. White
(*Assigning, Responding, Evaluating: A Writing Teacher's Guide*)

Designing well-constructed essay questions involves the same concerns and practices involved in designing all effective writing assignments. Because of the timed nature of essay exams, instructions must be as explicit as possible. Students need clear directions for the thinking tasks required by the assignment as well as complete information about the genre and format for presenting their answer. For example, the terms "compare and contrast" are more specific than "discuss." The directions to "write two blue-book page-length paragraphs" is more precise than to "write for fifteen minutes."

The following suggestions for assigning and evaluating essay exam questions may be useful:

1. Make sure that the code words in the question reflect the task you want students to perform. Be selective in choosing among words such as explain, analyze, evaluate, interpret. (See Appendix: "Terms Used in Assignment Instruction.")

2. Explain the meanings of the code words either immediately before students take the exam or during class instruction on taking essay exams. For example, the term "analysis" may call for both classification and interpretation.

3. Suggest guidelines for the approximate length and organization of the response, such as "Introduce your response by restating the question."

4. Alert students to typical pitfalls that often undermine the quality of an answer. For example, students often introduce answers with irrelevant background material.

5. Review techniques for preparing for and taking essay exams. (See the list on page 90.)

6. Give students practice in responding to essay questions. These sessions can also help students review course material and give instructors an opportunity to pilot essay questions to discover their degree of difficulty.

Evaluating Essay Exams

Grading essay questions should take into account the time limitations that may prevent some students from doing their best work. The planning, drafting, and revision process essential to good writing is truncated when taking an essay exam. Nevertheless, if the exam is well-constructed, students should have some time for planning and editing. If this is the case, then instructors should expect a well-organized response to the question, characterized for the most part by correct sentence structure. When grading essay questions, most instructors seem to assign more weight to content than to "presentation."

An effective essay exam is a powerful device for encouraging students to synthesize course material. The suggestions above are intended to help solve the problems that often discourage teachers from using them.

TAKING EXAMINATIONS

(Reprinted with permission from *More Learning in Less Time* by Norma B. Kahn 98–100)

Essay Examinations

1. Prepare to begin: Take slow deep breaths through your nose. Check the time (you watch by the clock) and ask whether it will be announced at all during the exam.

2. Underline key words in the directions and questions to focus your thinking, help you keep calm, and prevent you from trying to write before you are settled and organized.

3. Read through all questions first; jot down a few words that come to mind about each question you plan to answer (if there is a choice).

4. Budget your time.

   a. Consider the number of points given for each question, if this information is stated.

   b. Decide how much time you should allot for each answer.

   c. Allow time for a rough outline before writing each answer and for proofreading after completing the exam.

5. As a rule, answer the easiest question (or second easiest) first, to increase your confidence and give you more time to recall answers for the harder questions.

6. Jot down a rough outline from which to write your answer to each question.

   a. In a column, write key words and phrases related to points that you remember from lectures and from your reading and thinking for the course.

   b. Then think *beyond* these first ideas to new ideas that occur to you in response to the question; these ideas may be based on your own experiences and interests as well as the lectures and readings for the course.

   c. Number your points in the most appropriate order.

   d. If you run out of time in answering the question, copy points from your outline to complete your answer briefly.

7. Take care to answer precisely the question asked.

   a. Notice especially the limitation stressed by the instruction verb (list, analyze, compare).

   b. Form the first sentence by turning the question into a statement or by writing a thesis sentence that you will support with specific examples or evidence.

   c. Include a time frame, indicating, for example, whether an historical movement extended over decades or centuries.

   d. When in doubt, qualify your answers by using *approximate* times or dates and by including qualifying words (for example, "some" or "most," "usually" or "occasionally") in your statements.

   e. *Underline* the key phrases in your answer, so that the hurried exam reader will not miss a single one of them.

8. Begin a new paragraph for each point on your outline.

9. Support your main points with carefully chosen evidence or examples.

10. Abbreviate names or terms that you are likely to repeat frequently and include a code at the top of the page on which you first use the abbreviation (for example, T = Tchaikovsky; R = Revolution).

11. Write clearly, concisely, legibly. (If you prefer to type, inquire in advance about the possibility of typing your exam.)

12. Leave a space after each paragraph to allow for possible additions when you proofread or write your answers only on the front side of each page so that you can insert additions on the back of the preceding page.

13. Proofread your answer.

14. After you take an exam and it is returned to you, use it to determine how to study for and take exams more successfully.

C H A P T E R   3

Teaching
Materials
and
Student
Handouts

INTRODUCTION

These materials can be adapted to assignments in all disciplines. "Terms Used in Assignment Instructions" can help students to interpret the requirements of writing instructions. The other handouts, "Manuscript Form," "Plagiarism," and "Documentation"—APA/MLA, help students to understand conventions of presentation that apply to all academic writing. The "Peer-Review Guide Sheet" can be adopted for a variety of assignment types. The "Sample Responses to Student Drafts" can help instructors develop effective methods for responding to drafts.

TERMS USED IN ASSIGNMENT INSTRUCTIONS

analyze	give main divisions or elements, emphasizing essential parts
classify	arrange into main classes or divisions
compare	point out likenesses and differences (Sometimes the questioner intends to stress likenesses with the use of "compare" and may choose a combination of "compare and contrast" if both likenesses and differences are expected.)
contrast	point out differences
criticize	give your opinion as to good and bad features (with examples)
define	explain the meaning, distinguish from similar terms
discuss	examine in detail
evaluate	give your opinion of the value or validity
explain	make clear, give reasons for
illustrate	give one or more examples of
interpret	give the meaning or significance
justify	defend, show to be right
review	examine on a broad scale
summarize	go over the essentials briefly

A brief discussion of such terms helps students to understand assignments. Especially in the case of the exam essay, reading well is a necessary preliminary step to writing well.

For Students

MANUSCRIPT FORM

- Put your manuscript in acceptable form. Revise and proofread with care.

- Use the proper materials.

- Arrange your writing in clear and orderly fashion on the page.

- Unless you are given other instructions, follow these general practices:

1. *Margins:* Leave sufficient margins—about an inch and a half at the left and top, an inch at the right and at the bottom—to prevent a crowded appearance. The ruled vertical line on notebook paper marks the left margin.

2. *Indentation:* Indent the first lines of paragraphs uniformly.

3. *Pagination:* Use Arabic numerals—without parentheses or periods—in the upper right-hand corner.

4. *Title:* Do not put quotation marks around the title or underline it (unless it is a quotation or the title of a book), and use no period after the title. Capitalize the first and last words of the title and all other words except articles, coordinating conjunctions, prepositions, and the *to* in infinitives.

    When you do not use a title page, center the title on the page about an inch and a half from the top or on the first ruled line. Leave one blank line between the title and the first paragraph. When you do use a separate title page, include the following information attractively spaced: the title of your paper, your name, the course title and number, the instructor's name, and the date.

5. *Identification:* Usually papers carry the name of the student, the course title and number, the instructor's name, and the date. Often the number of the assignment is given.

For Students

PLAGIARISM

You must acknowledge all material quoted, paraphrased, or summarized from any work. Failing to cite a source, deliberately or accidentally, is plagiarizing—presenting as your own work the words or ideas of another. As the *MLA Handbook* (New York: Modern Language Assn., 1984) states,

> The most blatant form of plagiarism is to repeat as your own someone else's sentences, more or less verbatim. . . Other forms of plagiarism include repeating someone else's particularly apt phrase without appropriate acknowledgement, paraphrasing another person's argument as your own, and presenting another's line of thinking . . . as though it were your own.

After you have done a good deal of reading about a given subject, you will be able to distinguish between common knowledge in that field—facts, dates, and figures—and the distinctive ideas or interpretations of specific writers. When you use the ideas or information that these writers provide, be sure to cite the exact source of the material used.

NOT   In *Nineteen Eighty-Four*, doublethink is defined as the power of holding two contradictory beliefs in one's mind simultaneously, and accepting both of them. [undocumented copying]

BUT   In *Nineteen Eight-Four*, Orwell defines doublethink as "the power of holding two contradictory beliefs in one's mind simultaneously, and accepting both of them" (215). [Quotation marks enclose copied words, and the page number in parentheses cites the source.]

NOT   *Nineteen Eighty-Four* is Orwell's most ferocious propaganda. [an undocumented idea from the work of another writer]

BUT   *Nineteen Eighty-Four* has been called Orwell's most ferocious propaganda (Voorhees 87).

OR   Richard J. Voorhees states, "*Nineteen Eighty-Four* is his [Orwell's] fiercest piece of propaganda" (87).

If you are in doubt about whether you need to cite a source, the best policy is to cite it.

For Students

DOCUMENTATION

There is no one universally accepted way to document sources you use in your paper. Most instructors in the humanities prefer the MLA (Modern Language Association) format. Instructors in the natural and social sciences will usually prefer the APA (American Psychological Association) format. Here are examples of each.

Citations in APA Style

The basic elements of an APA citation are the author's last name, the year of publication, and the page number if the reference is to a specific passage in the source. If the author's name is mentioned in the text of the paper, the date alone or the date and the page number are given within parentheses.

Short quotation

One writer has stated, "Schools can be divided into private, public, and religious schools" (Bell, 1981, p. 217), an observation with which many organizations agree.

Long quotation

Bell (1981) has stated the following:

> "Schools can be divided into private, public, and religious schools. Each type is characterized by its curriculum and organizational structure" (p. 217).

Paraphrase

Bell (1981) suggested three categories for describing schools: private, public, and religious schools.

References

In APA style the alphabetical list of works cited is called "References." Observe details of indentation, spacing, and punctuation.

A book by one author

Bell, A. (1981) *Schools: Private, Public, Religious*. New York: Doubleday Co.

A book with two authors

Bell, A. & Klein, F. (1981). *Schools and the Community.* New York: Doubleday Co.

Journal article

Bell, A. (1980)."Schools and how we view them." *Journal of Teacher Education, 107,* 355–369.

Citations in the MLA Style

Endnotes are used to provide additional commentary on information in text, to list several sources, or to refer readers to additional sources. Otherwise, cite quotations as follows:

Short quotation

Use parenthetical references (in text) in one of three ways:

1. Cite author's last name and page number(s) of source in parentheses: One critic argues that Dreiser was "always concerned with social issues" (Stern 27).

2. Use author's last name in your sentence and place only the page number of your source in parentheses: Stern states that Dreiser was "always concerned with social issues" (27).

3. Give the author's last name when citing the entire work (rather than a specific section or passage) and omit any parenthetical references: Stern argues that Dreiser was primarily a social novelist.

Long quotation

Quoting a long passage, indent on left only, do not use quotation marks, provide a lead-in sentence, and place the page number of the source at the end of the quote after the final period.

Joyce Stern suggests that Dreiser was often describing specific social problems in New York:

> In his characters, plots, and settings, Dreiser highlighted many of the problems of the poor and dispossessed; his tales of the frustration and suffering of the weak and the powerless

often include accurate, detailed descriptions of actual situations many people in New York faced. (163)

List of works cited

Use a separate sheet; place in alphabetical order by last name; indent second and subsequent lines (not first).

Sample Entries

A book by one author

Stern, Joyce. *Theodore Dreiser.* New York: St. Martins Press, 1983.

A book with an editor

Bond, Charles, ed. *The Letters of Theodore Dreiser.* New York: St. Martins Press, 1983.

A work in an anthology

Smith, John. "Dreiser on the City." *Dreiser and New York.* Ed. Alice Benson. 2nd ed. New York: Macmillan, 1984: 17–26.

Journal article

Smith, Mary. "Dreiser and Women." *Short Fiction Studies* 54 (1992): 48–57.

FOR ADDITIONAL INFORMATION, SEE *THE MLA HANDBOOK.*

(Note: APA and MLA models are fictitious.)

PEER REVIEW GUIDE SHEET

Author:

Reviewer:

Title:

Draft #

Assignment #

1. What is your general reaction to the paper? Please explain.

2. What is the main point of the paper? What is the author trying to say?

3. Identify additional important ideas in the paper. List them.

4. Is there enough information in the paper to support major ideas? If not, explain where more information is needed.

5. Identify information that is irrelevant. Explain why.

SAMPLE RESPONSES TO STUDENT DRAFTS

The following paper and excerpts from two other papers were written in response to an assignment in Community Health Nursing, a course in the School of Nursing. The assignment required students to write a summary of the contents of the first four weeks of the course for the purpose of informing a nursing student unfamiliar with the course material. Students could choose the form in which they presented the information.

Each paper includes sample marginal and end-comments written to guide revision of the papers (see Chapter 1, "Assignment-Related Instruction").

Paper #1: Student A

Community Health Nursing is designed in such a way that the Regis-

Is this   tered Nurse will spend time working in the community and with indi-
usage   vidual families in the community. The nurse should see herself as a
common
for   change agent who will identify aggregates at risk for illness and prema-
'patients'?
ture death. Time will be spent working with community leaders and

SP

other health groups to hopefully make changes that are accommadating

to the community.

Community Health Nursing is focused on primary prevention,

protection, and health promotion. Members of the community are

encouraged to participate in health planning, self help, and to assume

personal responsibility for personal health habits which promote health

and a safe environment.

Community health nursing isn't a new concept. it has evolved over a
check
punctuation long period of time. Community Health Nursing developed in three stages:

The District Nurse Stage: In the 1860's with voluntary home care for

the poor since they couldn't afford hospitalization.

How are
the stages
connected

The Public Health Stage: 1900–1970: This period was characterized by a consciousness of the general public and its health care. The family

became the primary care givers.

Community Health Nursing Stage: 1970–present.

word choice? This stage began around 1970 and is still present. Its practice

priorities are prevention, protection, and promotion. The nursing

process and valuing process (to value something is to judge it worthy)

guide Community Health Nursing Practice.

Instructor's Comment:

Dear Student A

Your summary includes much of the material we covered in class. However, a student who is not in the class will need some additional information to recognize that this is a summary of the first four weeks, such as which material was emphasized during that period. Also, your summary is difficult to read because paragraphs are short and are not connected with transition sentences. Stop in for a conference if you need some help revising the paper.

◆ ◆ ◆ ◆ ◆

Paper #2: Student B

Dear Fran,

The final course in Nursing at La Salle is quite challenging. The past

four weeks have served as an introduction to the balance of the

semester's work. The instructor has based her material on three broad

themes. The first theme stressed in the course is the concept of perceiv-

ing public health nursing from a general systems theory perspective.

Another important theme of this course concerns the process of defining

Are these the same? public health nursing as an area of nursing practice. The final course

theme is the concept of viewing the environment (or community) as both the cause and the possible solution to the health care problems which threaten its inhabitants.

Perceiving public health nursing from a general systems theory perspective is consistent with the conceptual framework of the entire nursing program at La Salle University. This framework is founded on the belief that various systems of people, groups, and social forces are interrelated; the actions of one system will affect all other systems with which it interacts. Furthermore, any system is both more complex and contains more information than the sum of its individual parts. (The author continues to give a complete analysis of the three themes).

good transition!

Instructor's Comment:

Dear Student B

   Your summary is quite successful because it not only focuses on the overall content of the first four weeks but also identifies important themes linking the material. Also, you place the course content within the con-text of the curriculum, an important connection for your audience, stu-dents who have not yet taken the course. Also, your comment about the course being quite challenging brings in the "human factor" and pre-vents the writing from sounding stilted. Good job!

Paper #3: Student C

With the beginning of class the course syllabus and course require-ments were reviewed. I found there to be special import on the neces-sity of completing all the readings.

   We began discussing the ANA newsletter which is a position paper on the definition and role of public health nursing in the delivery of health care. The topic was to be continued later. There seemed to be too much class discussion at this point.   **I'm not sure what you mean.**

Separate into two sentences. Hard to read.

Seeing different parts of the population as aggregates was also a high priority of this lecture, and linked with this was the recognition of the health care need outside an institutional framework, yet without labeling the nurse that functions in this area as having a specialty. Also in this session we were introduced to the Environmental Health Model. (The author continues to organize the information by each lecture.)

Instructor's Comment:

Dear Student C

Your essay includes much information we reviewed during the first four weeks of class. However, a student who is not in the class will want to know which material was emphasized and how the major themes of the content of the first four weeks were organized, rather than what was covered in each session. Base the organization of the paper on the logic of the content rather than the content of each lecture. Stop in for a conference if you need help revising the paper.

C H A P T E R 4

Designing a Comprehensive Writing Program

In "What Do You Need to Start and Sustain a Writing-Across-the Curriculum Program?" McLeod and Soven argue that to launch a comprehensive writing program the writing program administrator or committee charged with the task of improving writing instruction must have the imprimatur of the administration and the faculty. The administration should demonstrate its support by publicly affirming the importance of the program, appointing a coordinator, providing a budget, and creating an administrative structure, such as an advisory committee to oversee the program—and by not expecting change to happen overnight. (28–31)

Given the fact that WAC programs involve comprehensive curricular change, they take time to develop. Successful programs must grow through faculty consensus and dialogue. Most writing program administrators agree that it is best to begin reforming a writing program through faculty development, rather than through a top-down approach. Administrative fiat does not seem to work. Depending on the size of the faculty, it can take several years of workshops before any widespread changes in classroom practices can be detected and curricular change starts to take shape. There should be a reward system for faculty who participate in writing across the curriculum workshops. Preferably they should receive a stipend and, more important, acknowledgment by the administration of their efforts to improve their teaching.

A vital resource needed to create successful WAC programs are support systems for both students and faculty. A writing center can provide tutoring for students who need one-on-one help with their writing. Curriculum-based peer tutoring programs, in which peer tutors are assigned to individual courses to read the drafts of all students' papers in that course, can underscore the importance of revision as part of the writing process. These programs are often called "Writing Fellows" or "Writing Associate" Programs.

When a significant number of the faculty have been introduced to writing across the curriculum theory and practice, then curriculum revisions to strengthen the writing program can be introduced. For example, a writing emphasis course requirement for all students or a specialized course in advanced writing in the major may be implemented. At the same time, the freshman composition program should be revised to become an integral part of the comprehensive writing program.

Student publications that include writing in all disciplines can be developed to highlight excellence in writing. Faculty can encourage students to submit their good papers for these campus-wide publications.

From the beginning, procedures for evaluating the writing program should be put into place. Formative evaluation can help a writing program remain responsive to the needs of faculty and students. For example, faculty should evaluate the effectiveness of writing across the curriculum workshops. Students and faculty should evaluate peer tutoring programs. Portfolio assessment can help gather information on students' writing experiences.

For a more extended treatment of the development of and evaluation of comprehensive writing programs see *Writing Across the Curriculum: A Guide to Developing Programs* by McLeod and Soven.

THE LA SALLE UNIVERSITY WRITING PROGRAM

This description of the writing program at La Salle University is not intended as a model for all schools but as an example of one institution's efforts to design a comprehensive program. Many of its components could be adapted for both high school and colleges.

The university offers a multifaceted writing experience, the foundation of which is the freshman composition program administered through the English Department. The freshman program is supplemented by the writing emphasis course requirement, taken by juniors and seniors in all majors. In addition, the university demonstrates its commitment to strong writing in all the disciplines through a vigorous writing component in the foundation courses, the Writing Fellows Program, the Writing Across the Curriculum Faculty Development Project, and the Sheekey Writing Center.

English Department

The Freshman Composition Program

The La Salle University Freshman Composition Program integrates instruction in writing and reading skills and emphasizes the kinds of writing required of students in their other studies. Students learn strategies for planning, drafting, revising, and editing their writing.

College Writing I begins with a review of fundamental skills at the sentence and paragraph level. However, by the end of the semester, students will have had some experience writing essays that use texts as evidence. (Some students have this course waived because of their SAT scores and high school records.)

College Writing II provides instruction in summarizing, analyzing, and critiquing readings. In addition, all students write a brief research paper after an introduction to the library. Instruction emphasizes careful documentation of sources to avoid plagiarism.

The English Writing Major combines a strong liberal arts background in literature with offerings in creative writing, journalism, editing, desktop publishing, business writing, and technical writing.

The Communication Writing Track combines core studies in media and specialized courses in writing. Both the Communication and English programs feature, for qualified juniors and seniors, internships in professional settings in and around Philadelphia and on campus.

Writing University Wide

The Foundation Courses

The foundation courses are most directly related to La Salle's aims and traditions as a liberal arts university. In addition to those in writing and literature, each of the remaining foundation courses—history, computer science, religion, philosophy, science, and social science—contains its own written component.

The Writing Emphasis Course Requirement

Students are required to take a Writing Emphasis Course in their major discipline at the junior/senior level. Writing Emphasis Courses require a writing project approved by each major department.

Faculty Workshops

Faculty workshops are offered on the basic principles of designing and evaluating writing assignments and on the relationship between critical thinking and writing. Special topics are introduced related to faculty interest, such as "Developing Essay Test Questions" and "Alternatives to the Term Paper."

Week-long workshops for which the faculty receive a stipend are held during the summer. Day-long workshops are held periodically during the academic year. Faculty from all departments in the School of Arts and Sciences, the School of Business Administration, and the Department of Nursing are invited to attend.

In addition, the WAC director works on a personal basis with interested faculty.

Student Publications: The Essay Contest

Students from all departments are invited to submit papers written in their courses to the annual across-the-disciplines essay contest. The six winning essays are published in a booklet, *Writing Across the Disciplines: Writing Project Essay Contest Winners.* Faculty are urged to encourage students who write exemplary papers to submit them for consideration.

Peer Tutoring Programs: The Writing Fellows Program

Twenty-five students are involved in the Writing Fellows Program each year. Students apply to become Writing Fellows by submitting samples of their writing and attending an interview. Many students apply because their instructors have recommended that they consider the program.

Although the deadline for submissions to both the Writing Fellows Program and the Writing Contest is **February** entries may be submitted throughout the year. Applications are available in the English Department Office.

All faculty who teach in the day division can request a Writing Fellow for one of their courses.

The Sheekey Writing Center

The Sheekey Writing Center offers La Salle students individual instruction in all aspects of writing—from grammar and mechanics, to sentence, paragraph, and whole paper skills, to preparation of resumes and statements for graduate and professional schools. The center also offers workshops in reading and study skills. Both professional and peer tutors assist students on a drop-in or referral basis.

WRITING ACROSS THE CURRICULUM: RECOMMENDED READING AND WORKS CITED

Bazerman, Charles. *The Informed Writer: Using Sources in the Disciplines.* 2nd ed. Boston: Houghton Mifflin, 1985.

Behrens, Laurence and Leonard Rosen. *Writing and Reading Across the Curriculum.* 2nd ed. Boston: Little Brown & Co., 1985.

Britton, James, et al. *The Development of Writing Abilities (11–18).* London: Macmillan Publishers, 1975.

Bruffee, Kenneth. *A Short Course in Writing.* Cambridge, Mass.: Winthrop Publishers, Inc., 1980.

Connolly, Paul and Teresa Vilardi, eds. *Writing to Learn Mathematics and Science.* New York: Teachers College Press, 1989.

Corbett, Edward. *The Little Rhetoric and Handbook.* 2nd ed. Glenview, IL: Scott Foresman and Co., 1982.

Didion, Joan. "Why I Write," *Eight Modern Essays.* Ed. William Smart. New York: St. Martins Press, 1980.

Emig, Janet. "Writing as a Mode of Learning." *College Composition and Communication,* 28 (1977): 21–28.

Fulwiler, Toby. *The Journal Book.* Portsmouth, NH: Boynton, 1987.

Fulwiler, Toby and Art Young, eds. *Programs that Work: Models and Methods of Writing Across the Curriculum.* Portsmouth, NH: Boynton-Cook, 1990.

Gaudiani, Claire. *Teaching Composition in the Foreign Language Curriculum.* Washington D.C.: Center for Applied Linguistics, 1981.

Griffith, Kelley. *Writing Essays about Literature.* New York: Harcourt Brace Jovanovich, Inc., 1982.

Griffin, C. Williams, ed. *Teaching Writing in All Disciplines.* San Francisco: Jossey-Bass, 1982.

Hairston, Maxine. *Successful Writing: A Rhetoric for Advanced Composition.* New York: W.W. Norton & Co., 1981.

Hale, Connie J. and Susan Wyche-Smith, dirs. *Using Student Writing Groups.* Tacoma, WA: Wordshop Productions, Inc., 1988.

Harris, Muriel. *Teaching One-to-One.* Urbana, Ill., National Council of Teachers of English, 1986.

Harty, Kevin and John Keenan. *Writing for Business and Industry.* New York: Macmillan Publishing Co., 1987.

Holder, Carol and Andrew Moss. *Improving Student Writing.* Pomona, CA: California State Polytechnic University, 1982.

Kahn, Norma B. *More Learning in Less Time.* 3rd ed. Berkeley, CA: Ten Speed Press, 1989.

Kinneavy, James. "The Liberal Arts and the Current Moral and Political Crisis," unpublished paper, delivered at La Salle University, 1989.

Kinneavy, James. et al. *Writing in the Liberal Arts Tradition.* New York: Harper and Row, 1985.

Kloss, Robert. ed. O. Paterson, N. J.: William Patterson College, 1985.

Larson, Richard. "Teaching Before We Judge: Planning Assignments in Composition," *The Writing Teacher's Sourcebook,* ed. by Gary Tate and Edward J. Corbett. New York: Oxford University Press, 1981.

Larson, Richard, with assistance of Eve Zarin and Carol Sicherman. *Writing in the Academic and Professional Disciplines.* New York: Herbert H. Lehman College, 1983.

Lutzker, Marilyn. *Research Projects for College Students: What to Write Across the Curriculum.* Westport, CT: Greenwood, 1988.

Maimon, Elaine, et al. eds. *"Thinkings and Writings: The Classical Tradition."* Thinking, Reasoning and Writing. eds. Maimon et. al. New York: Longman, 1989.

Maimon, Elaine et al. *Writing in the Arts and Sciences.* Cambridge, MA: Withrop Publishers, Inc., 1981.

Mcleod, Suan H. and Margot Soven, eds. *Writing Across the Curriculum: A Guide to Developing Programs.* Newbury Park, CA: SAGE Publications, Inc., 1992.

Pechenik, Jan. *Writing About Biology.* Boston: Little Brown and Co., 1987.

Shaughnessy, Mina. *Errors and Expectations.* New York: Oxford University Press, 1977.

Walvoord, Barbara Fassler. *Helping Students Write Well: A Guide for Teachers in All Disciplines.* 2nd ed., New York: MLA, 1986.

White, Edward M. *Assigning, Responding, Evaluating.* 2nd ed. New York: St. Martin's Press, 1992.

Zinnser, William. *Writing to Learn.* New York: Harper, 1988.